BORN TO BE ALL OF ME

*Moving Out of Self-Abandonment
Into Authentic Embodiment*

AMBER SUSA

**LANDON
HAIL**
PRESS

Copyright© 2024 Amber Susa
All Rights Reserved

This book or any portion thereof may not be reproduced or used in any manner without the express written permission of the publisher, except for the use of brief quotations in a book review.

Paperback ISBN: 978-1-959955-34-4
Hardback ISBN: 978-1-959955-35-1
Cover design by Rich Johnson, Spectacle Photo
Cover photo: Mary Lou Sandler, 3cubedstudios.com

Published by Landon Hail Press

Although the author and publisher have made every effort to ensure the accuracy and completeness of information contained in this book, we assume no responsibility for errors, inaccuracies, omissions, or any inconsistency herein. Any slights on people, places, or organizations are unintentional. The material in this book is provided for educational purposes only. No responsibility for loss occasioned to any person or corporate body acting or refraining to act as a result of reading material in this book can be accepted by the author or publisher.

I dedicate this book to anyone who has ever dimmed their light in an attempt to fit in and belong. Anyone who has given their power away and become a disempowered version of themselves in an attempt to feel safe and be loved. Anyone who has forgotten the truth of who they are and has numbed the pain of forgetting with behaviors and habits that bring deep shame.

I dedicate this book to anyone who is ready for a new beginning... ready to take back their power and say yes to the call of their soul. Anyone who knows they are here for more and is ready to walk courageously into the version of themselves they know they were born to be.

I dedicate this book to my children, Dawson and Will, that they may never forget the truth of who they are: expressions of the Divine, here to BE love and manifest the desires of their heart. It is my deepest wish and prayer that by me saying yes to the call of my soul and modeling for my children a woman who walks in faith and Divine purpose, they will know what is possible for them.

I believe with every fiber of my being that we are all here with a unique purpose and mission; that our natural gifts, talents, and deepest heart's desires are clues to the fulfillment of this mission. I believe anything is possible. I believe in magic and miracles. I believe in love. I believe in me. I believe in you.

CONTENTS

Foreword	1
Chapter 1: Awe and Wonder	3
Writing prompt	4
Unapologetic and Free	5
Writing Prompt	8
Chapter 2: Adapting to Fit In	9
I Need to Dim My Light So People Will Like Me	9
The Battle Between Ego and Soul	10
Attachment Vs. Authenticity	13
Writing Prompt	15
My First "Love"	15
Journal Entry: A Letter To Brown Bronco	18
We Are Loyal to the Beliefs in our Family Systems	21
Chapter 3: The Weight of Carrying Someone Else's Pain	23
Being Sensitive Is Not A Compliment	23
I Feel Different	24
Journal Entry	25
Journal Entry – Early Motherhood	27
Journal Entry 2015 - Running on Empty	30
Journal Entry - Early in my Healing Journey	32
Journal Entry - Early Motherhood	34
Journal Entry 2015	38
The Pain of Self-Abandonment	38
Born To Fly	45
How Patterns Are Born	47
Illusions and Stories	55
Journal Entry - March 7, 2019	57
Journal Entry - June 2019	60
Writing Prompt	65

Chapter 4: Tired of Living a Lie	**66**
Oprah Winfrey & Deepak Chopra	69
21-Day Meditation Challenge: Perfect Health	69
A Memory Rises To The Surface	72
More Synchronicities	75
Journal Entry	80
Journal Entry	81
Journal Entry - Sunday, April 5, 2020	83
Journal Entry - Tuesday, April 7, 2020	85
Journal Entry - Wednesday, April 8, 2020	86
Journal Entry Thursday, April 9, 2020	87
Chapter 5: The Quest to Understand	**90**
There's No Such Thing As "Perfect"	90
Journal Entry Tuesday, July 30, 2019	98
Feel It to Heal It	98
Writing Prompt	101
Uncovering Subconscious Beliefs	101
Daydreaming with Ego and Soul	103
Journal Entry: Creating My One-Woman Show	105
Chapter 6: Strong Enough to Embrace the Truth	**107**
Journal Entry - Sunday, April 28, 2019	111
Journal Entry - April 12, 2018	113
Journal Entry - Sunday, June 30, 2019	113
The Divorce	115
Journal Entry - June 2, 2020	115
Journal Entry - June 9, 2020	116
Journal Entry - June 10, 2020	117
Journal Entry - June 20, 2020	117
Journal Entry - June 21, 2020	117
Journal Entry - June 22, 2020	118
Journal Entry - June 24, 2020	118
Journal Entry - June 30, 2020	118
Journal Entry - July 4, 2020	118
Journal Entry - July 9, 2020	119
Journal Entry - July 10, 2020	119
Journal Entry - August 10, 2020	120

Journal Entry - August 11, 2020	120
Journal Entry - August 30, 2020	121
Journal Entry - September 8, 2020	121
Journal Entry: The Inner Knowing 2021	122
Learning to Trust the Inner Voice Again	122
Uncertainty and Faith	123
Journal Entry - Thursday, September 24, 2020	124
Journal Entry - October 15, 2020	125
Riding the Waves	127
Journal Entry - Monday, November 16, 2020	127
It's All About Alignment	128
Chapter 7: Helping to Create the Shift	**132**
Waking Up and Becoming the Embodied Woman	132
A Vision for the New	133
Climbing Out of the Deep Well of Darkness	133
Writing Prompt	139
Trusting Divine Timing	141
Journal Entry - February 16, 2021	142
Creating A New Reality Based on Personal Truth And Sovereignty	144
Writing Prompt	145
Journal Entry - January 2021	145
A Message From Spirit	146
Journal Entry - February 2023	148
Journal Entry - March 7, 2023	148
Journal Entry - March 12, 2023	149
Journal Entry - April 11, 2023	149
Journal Entry - June 1, 2023	151
Journal Entry - July 2, 2023	152
April 15, 2023 - The Great Mother Poem	153
A Message from Spirit	155
Journal Entry - May 12, 2023	156
Journal Entry - June 13, 2023	157
Authenticity, Alignment, Allowing	158
Alignment First, Then Action	164
Gratitude Meditation Practice	165

Manage Your Mood	166
Journal Entry - July 2, 2023	167
Embodiment Challenge	167
Diving Into New Beliefs	168
Heart's Desires and I AM Affirmations	169
The Divine Feminine	172
Writing Prompt	178
Acknowledgments	**182**
About the Author	**184**

Foreword

The gap between your soul purpose, what your soul loves, and the amount of time you spend doing it will be the size of your suffering. It is a known fact that the further away one lives from their true selves, the greater the distance they are from living in ease, freedom, and health. Life's example of harmony.

However, in a world that emphasizes production over quality of life, consumption over expression, the task to achieve harmony has become our greatest challenge. This conflict shows up in our relationships, finances, and physical and emotional health as disease.

Yet harmony is what we are all here to experience and bring to the world.

Yes.

We are all being called to heal by the evidence of collective discord, division, and disease. As a studied mystic, licensed holistic psychotherapist, practitioner of root-cause healing, transformational speaker, and the artist of my own healing from debilitating disease, CPTSD, I understand the healing process has more to do with deconstructing what isn't true in order to create space for a remembrance of the soul. The most divine expression of the mind of the universe, embodied wisdom, and love. The journey of our healing is our gift to receive and give.

Amber puts the *whole* in holistic health. Her healing journey is nothing short of miraculous. The storytelling within this book draws us in immediately, because we all can see a little (or a lot) of ourselves in her story. The vulnerability and raw open honesty bring all aspects of our human essence to life. She is a living, breathing version of a healer. Her energy is infectious and her Faith muscle is strong!

Sharon Land, LPC, NCC holistic psychotherapist
Speaker, High-Performance Mentor
Author of Bestseller, *The Healer's Journey*

Chapter 1
Awe and Wonder

It was Christmas morning, 1982, in Long Beach, California. I was seven years old. I waited in the hallway with my ten-month-old sister, Carrie, squealing with joyful anticipation. Santa had always been so generous, and I couldn't wait to see what he delivered this year.

I wasn't allowed to walk into the living room until everything was ready. The stage had to be set... picture-perfect fire burning in the fireplace; stuffed stockings placed on the hearth, too heavy to hang from the mantle; presents under the tree spilling out into the middle of the living room; and Nat King Cole singing, "Chestnuts Roasting on an Open Fire" in the background. *Leave It To Beaver* perfection, complete with a handsome handlebar-mustache-wearing dad and a beautiful mom with luscious blonde locks.

My dad had that old-school Panasonic VHS video recorder the size of a toaster. He set it up on the tripod and pressed record, letting it run for hours, capturing all the important moments and the moments in between.

I relished every bit of it, opening each gift with such delight, face lit up, eyes opened wide, jaw dropped in amazement. With every single gift, I looked at my parents, bursting with enthusiasm, and exclaimed, "Colored paper... It's what I always wanted."

Every gift was "what I always wanted." I was in such awe of these miraculous gifts. A book of colored paper, a box of colored pencils... With each gift, I became more and more filled with awe and wonder. How did Santa get it so perfectly every year, delivering everything I wanted and more?

And then, it was time to open the next gift... The anticipation, as I struggled to open the box, my parents watching with such eagerness to see what reaction this one would get.

I shrieked with my raspy little pre-tonsillectomy voice, barely able to get the words out of my mouth, "It's... It's... It's... It's a *PIP*! It's a PIP! It goes like stamp! So, I can write my name on the colored paper."

PIP Printing was a Southern California printing company that made personal stamps. I got a PIP stamp with my name on it, which I thought was the most incredible thing I had ever seen.

This is the girl I am remembering. This is the girl I was born to be. This is my True Self. She is light. She is love. She lives in awe and wonder.

Writing prompt

What does a life filled with awe and wonder feel like?

When do we lose that, and why?

Imagine if we could still access that beautiful innocence of our child self, seeing every gift with such appreciation and amazement. Allowing ourselves to receive.

Take a moment to reflect on a time in your life when you experienced awe and wonder. Close your eyes, take a couple deep breaths, and be with this feeling.

∽∽∽∽

My childhood Christmases are out of a movie. My parents seriously over did it! Perhaps they were trying to make up for what they didn't have, growing up. Neither of them had ideal childhoods.

My dad's mom died when he was seven. And my mother's parents had an awful divorce when she was fourteen. Bless their hearts, when they decided to start a family of their own, they vowed to be the perfect family... And we were the "perfect" family.

Unapologetic and Free

One of the most significant experiences of my life, and one that I return to, whenever I need help remembering who I am, happened at the age of ten.

For as long as I can remember, I have loved being on stage... performing, dancing, acting, singing. It came from a natural place, a place deep inside me, my soul. It felt like I was born to be there.

One day after school, my mom was watching a television talk show called *3-3-0 with Steve Edwards and Mary Fran*. This particular episode, their guest was Mary Grady, a top children's agent.

They made an announcement about a "kiddie cattle call" they were having, where the winner would get representation from one of the largest children's agencies in the entertainment industry. I told my mom I wanted to go and audition.

At the time, my only experience "performing" was at my gymnastics meets and dance recitals at the local parks and rec department. But I was performing regularly in my living room and in front of the mirrored closet doors in my parent's bedroom, so I felt sufficiently prepared. I would belt out Donna Summer, with my hair-brush microphone in hand, to my make-believe audience of thousands.

It never dawned on me that I didn't have enough experience. I didn't doubt my abilities; I knew how much I loved to perform, and that was all that mattered. I was thrilled when my mom agreed to take me! One thing is for certain: my parents were my biggest cheerleaders and gave me every opportunity to follow my dreams.

My mom's parents were both in the entertainment industry as children. My Nana was a stunning acrobat and dancer, and my grandfather was a successful child actor. I guess, because of their negative experiences in the industry, they decided my mom was never allowed to take any kind of performance-related classes.

So, when I came into this world, a born performer, it was the perfect opportunity for both of us. My mom's inner child got to experience something she hadn't been allowed to, through me, and she also got to give me experiences and opportunities that her mom wasn't able to give her. Luckily for me, I got to follow my dream of being a performer, something I felt I was born for.

The day of the contest, my mom and I drove to Hollywood. My only preparation was being me and feeling excited. When we arrived, there were thousands of kids and their parents, lined up around the block, waiting in hopeful anticipation of being the next child star.

We waited for hours. I was 10... the age my daughter is now... I can imagine I was quite antsy and impatient. But finally, it was my turn. My chance to dazzle the important grown-ups.

I did a little dance routine, a couple of gymnastics moves, answered some questions, and read the lines on the paper they handed me. I loved it! I was a natural. They put me in a group with the other kids who got a callback and asked me to wait.

I made it through another round and was asked to schedule an appointment at Mary Grady's office the following week. A few meetings later, it was announced. They'd chosen one girl and one boy as the winners of the contest. The winners would get representation with the Mary Grady Talent Agency and make an appearance with Mary herself on the television show, *3-3-0*, where the contest had been announced.

I won the contest! I was the girl, chosen out of thousands. They saw something special in me. I wasn't the prettiest, not the most talented, and certainly not the most experienced... But my spirit was bright, and my energy was magnetic. I was a bright light who believed in herself, and somewhere deep inside, I knew it was my destiny.

That time in my life was one of my last memories of me feeling that level of belief and trust in myself, my deep inner knowing. Life has a way of stealing that knowing; experiences begin to erode the natural confidence of a child. Self-doubt, comparison, and the need to belong all begin to shape our connection to ourselves and to the people in our lives.

Writing Prompt

What do you love to do?

What risks would you take, if the only requirement was loving it?

What would you say yes to, if "no experience was necessary"?

Think back to a time before you worried about what other people thought. How would your life be different, if you didn't care what anyone else thought, and you made choices from a place of love and enthusiasm? From your deep inner knowing?

ઠેઠેઠેઠે

Chapter 2

Adapting to Fit In

I Need to Dim My Light So People Will Like Me

When I was twelve, I got the lead in my first musical. It was summer, and my mom had signed me up for the Long Beach Summer Youth Conservatory.

I had never done a musical, had never taken any singing lessons. And yet it felt so natural, so authentic. I was cast in the leading role of Daisy Mae in *Li'l Abner*. Huge theater, big stage, bright lights… It was magical. I can still close my eyes and feel the bright lights shining on my face as I sang my little carefree heart out.

The next year, I got the lead again. I was cast as Kim in *Bye Bye Birdie*. That year, however, wasn't nearly as magical. I found out that some of the other girls' moms had complained to the director about me being cast as the lead for the second year in a row.

"My daughter Megan is perfect for the role. It's not fair to the other girls. Two years in a row? It's not right…"

I was absolutely devastated. It was one of the first times I remember feeling it wasn't safe to be my full true self. That people might not like me, if I stood out too much. Getting the lead two years in a row upset people. And I couldn't stand the thought of upsetting people or having people not like me.

"Trauma is not what happens to you. Trauma is what happens inside you as a result of what happens to you. Trauma is a wound, and that wound persists. The trauma is not the circumstance… It's what you make the circumstance mean."

—Dr. Gabor Maté

I made the circumstance of the complaining moms mean it wasn't safe to shine. Their comments wounded me. I took it personally. I took it to mean that people don't like it when you are your authentic self and shine your bright light.

This became a theme throughout my life. I made a decision that I needed to dim my light in order for people to like me, accept me. This circumstance seemed to birth a new version of myself.

The Battle Between Ego and Soul

"Yo, Amber. The name is Ego. Listen, I'm here to protect you, keep you safe, help you belong. First of all, whatever you do, do not stand out! Don't get too much attention. Dim Your Light! Otherwise, people won't like you, and you'll be alone forever!"

Alone forever? *WTF*? Seems drastic, I know. But I have learned that my Ego likes to take drastic measures, when he feels threatened. It is his job to protect me, after all.

My Ego is like Joe Pesci's wise-guy mobster character in *Good Fellas*, buzzing around like an annoying gnat, constantly reminding me of all the things that could go wrong. He likes to paint a picture of all the worst-case scenarios, trying to convince me that making a wrong decision could get me whacked.

He also loves to remind me of all the reasons why I am a failure, laying out all the tangible evidence to prove his point. When I spend too much time listening to him, I feel like a loser and a letdown.

Throughout my life, it felt like there were two versions of me, two voices battling it out in my head. One was filled with awe and wonder, utterly optimistic and free, unapologetic about shining her light. And the other one constantly pointed out my flaws, comparing me to others, exceedingly concerned about fitting in. It was like I had an internal dimmer switch, and depending on who was winning the battle, I was either at full brightness or safely dimmed.

"Shrink! Turn down the volume. Just be like everyone else, Amber," Ego would remind me often.

It's painful, trying to be like everyone else. And confusing.

The other voice was much gentler and more encouraging, like Glinda the Good Witch in *The Wizard of Oz*. She is the voice of my Soul. She is wise and kind, a loving Fairy Godmother type who knows just what to say to make me feel calm and reassured.

"Just breathe and trust… You are exactly where you are supposed to be," she says.

When I am listening to Glinda, I feel confident and connected to the part of me who knows who I am and why I am here. I remember that it is safe to be me, my true self, all of me.

She lives in a utopian place like Oz, where the colors are bright and the landscape vast, with rolling green hills and big, beautiful flowers. And he lives in the seedy neighborhoods of Brooklyn, like in *Good Fellas*. One place feels safe and comforting, makes you want to sing like you're in the movie, *Sound of Music*, and one reminds you to keep your head on a swivel, because someone could jump you and take your purse any minute.

It can be very confusing... Which one is telling the truth?

It was hard to debate Ego's point, after my *Bye Bye Birdie* experience. He was clearly right. People don't like it when you shine too brightly. Standing out and being disliked wasn't something I was willing to risk. Ego won the battle for many years to come.

I morphed into what seemed acceptable, what helped me feel like I belonged. I spent years completely disconnected from my true self, choosing relationships from that disconnected place, struggling with addiction, dimming my light, and walking away from the things that brought me joy and lit my soul on fire. Always adapting and morphing, asleep to my truth, and always feeling like something was missing.

I have come to know what was missing... It was me. All of me!

We learn to associate being our authentic selves as a threat and a vehicle to being rejected. This pattern gets repeated throughout our lives. And we wonder why we feel so alone.

If you're not known, you're going to feel alone. It doesn't matter how many people surround you. You abandon your true nature and give up your need to authentically express yourself in order to feel safe and belong. But if you don't feel like the people you "belong" to really know you, you will feel alone. A vicious cycle that keeps you from having your needs met.

Attachment Vs. Authenticity

"People have two needs: attachment and authenticity. When authenticity threatens attachment, attachment trumps authenticity."

—Dr. Gabor Maté

Attachment can be defined as our natural human need to experience connection and a sense of belonging. Authenticity is our innate desire to authentically express and make decisions that align with our true self.

According to retired physician and best-selling author Dr. Gabor Maté, if acting as our true self threatens our sense of belonging, we will inevitably abandon our authentic self to experience the connection we are searching for and that we think will keep us safe.

"I belong everywhere I go, no matter where it is or who I'm with, as long as I never betray myself. And the minute I become who you want me to be, in order to fit in and make sure people like me, is the moment I no longer belong anywhere."

—Brene Brown

According to *New York Times* best-selling author and research professor Brene Brown, our sense of belonging ends as soon as we abandon our authentic self and adapt to fit in.

It turns out the sense of belonging we have desperately been searching for is impossible in this codependent, self-abandoning paradigm we have been living in. And this is why we are being called into a new, more fulfilling interdependent, self-honoring paradigm.

We are designed to be in relationship and community. And we are designed to uniquely express who we were born to be. In a perfect world, these two things can be fulfilled simultaneously. However, there are many instances when acting as one's true self triggers a negative response in another person, and we retract; a subconscious belief is born, and we decide it is not safe to be our true self. We abandon our need to authentically express and adapt in order to belong.

At some point in our childhood, we have an experience that tells us, in order to have one of our needs met, we must abandon the other. Our need to feel safe trumps every other need.

When you consider both Gabor Maté and Brene Brown's observations, it explains the real conundrum we humans find ourselves in.

We are constantly abandoning our true self in order to belong, but this act of self-abandonment takes away our sense of belonging. We end up in this loop of self-abandonment and people-pleasing; we pretzel ourselves into whomever we think people want us to be. And we end up feeling alone, confused, and unfulfilled.

According to Vienna Pharaon in her book, *The Origins of You,* the path of authenticity and living authentically means that your choices and actions align with your core beliefs, values, and true self. It means you choose that path, even when there are consequences from the world around you.

When there is a belonging wound at play, it's pretty hard to choose authenticity. Living authentically is uncomfortable if you haven't been living that way.

This is why I am writing this book. I need to have this conversation... my soul with your soul... so we can bravely walk into this new space of authentic alignment and belonging to ourselves.

Writing Prompt

What does life look like without co-dependency?

What do relationships look like in this new paradigm?

What does it look like when generational trauma is healed and patterns are broken?

This is what I am discovering. This is the question my soul is asking me to find the answer to. And I want to share it with you.

ఈఈఈఈ

My First "Love"

I met my "first love" at the age of fifteen. For the purpose of anonymity, we'll call him Brown Bronco.

My family had taken a trip to Lake Arrowhead to go skiing, and one night we went out for pizza. There he was... a toe-headed blond, with blue eyes and a smile that made my heart melt. He and his buddy approached us while we waited for our pizza.

I'd been allowed to bring my friend Tiffany, so I guess it was less intimidating than if I had just been with my parents and eight-year-old sister.

He casually introduced himself and confidently invited us to come hang out at their cabin down the road, if it was okay with my parents. The combination of his angelic face, Eddie Haskell vibes, and the fact that I had never done anything that would cause my parents to doubt my judgment made my parents feel comfortable enough to say yes.

They agreed to drop us off at the cabin and pick us up a couple hours later. We didn't have cell phones at the time, so God forbid something had gone terribly wrong—I'd have had no way of letting them know. I guess we were all more naïve back then.

The boys were staying at a nearby cabin without parents. They were a little older... sixteen and seventeen. They were drinking beers and smoking pot. They offered us wine coolers, but we emphatically declined. The only time I had ever tasted alcohol was when my parents had the occasional after-dinner Kahlua, and I would suck on their ice cubes when they were done. So, there was no way I was going to drink with these boys.

I had never even been around marijuana, so I had no idea that's what I smelled when we walked into their cabin. We had a nice time, listened to some music, chatted about whatever teenagers chat about... and I was in love. Or at least what I thought love felt like.

We exchanged numbers and agreed to meet up when we were both back in Long Beach. Oh yes, did I mention that he also lived in Long Beach, only a few miles away from my house? So, clearly it was destiny that we be together.

On the drive home from Lake Arrowhead, destiny was confirmed when I looked out the passenger window of my mom's white Volvo station wagon and saw him driving this big, brown Bronco.

When I met him, I was acting, dancing, singing… doing the things I was born to do. But the more I "fell in love" or, truthfully, fell infatuated, I found myself wanting to spend more time with him and less time doing anything that didn't involve him. I slowly began to pull away from all these things I loved most. It didn't feel like I was abandoning myself; it felt like I was falling in love and losing interest in other things.

In this relationship with Brown Bronco, I did not honor myself. I gave away my power. He cheated on me all the time, and I did not love myself enough to leave. Instead, I chose to numb with drugs and alcohol, which helped numb the pain of becoming a disempowered version of myself. It also helped to keep me in denial, because I wasn't ready to leave.

I gave up acting. I quit the singing group I was in with the girls at my dance studio. This was right before all the girl bands and boy bands became a huge thing, and we were on that trajectory.

Singing and dancing are two of my most favorite things, and yet I felt conflicted… I was missing out on being a "normal" teenager and spending time with my boyfriend. Over time, I found myself wanting to pull away from my studio and my dance friends and wanting to spend more time with him and my other "normal" friends.

I'll never forget the time on my high school senior trip, when my class was going to Puerto Vallarta. I wasn't going to be able to go on the trip, because my singing group had rehearsals and a show. I so badly didn't want to miss out on this "normal life" experience. So, I decided to quit my singing group. I convinced myself I didn't want to do it anymore. I gave it up and went on this trip. I drank a ton of alcohol and smoked a ton of weed.

I guess I had fun. I thought I had fun. I felt a sense of belonging with my high school friends that I didn't normally feel. But this abandonment of self, so I might experience a sense of belonging, became a pattern I would repeat throughout my life, to the detriment of my well-being.

ৡৡৡৡ

Journal Entry: A Letter To Brown Bronco

I was a beautiful girl who sparkled and shined her light. I met you and everything fell apart... I became obsessed, infatuated. I felt inferior, begging for your attention and affection. Following you around all of Long Beach, meeting you at any damn party you were going to be at, just for the opportunity to be near you, in the hopes you'd want to be near me. I felt so fucking pathetic. No self-esteem, no self-respect.

A wounded boy, a party boy, a womanizer... So much uncertainty and insecurity were born in me. How I felt in the moments I got to be with you felt worth it. Your smile, the way you looked at me—my heart melted, and I did anything to be with you.

I ignored red flags. I only saw the good in you. I only focused on how I felt when I was with you. What about the times I wasn't with you? The times I waited at home, waiting for your call, replaying all of your voice messages just to hear your voice, meeting you anytime you dangled a carrot, dropping everything and anything, just to be with you.

I was persistent. I wanted you, I wanted you to be my boyfriend. I chased you around like a pathetic puppy dog, and finally you came to my sixteenth birthday party, and I "dazzled" you—this is what you told me. I dazzled you. The high I felt being chosen by you was immeasurable.

The first time I smoked pot was when you kissed Michelle P at the party on Ocean and Cherry, next to the park... Fuck it. Fuck it all... I'll get high because you picked another girl tonight. I'll hurt myself because you don't want me tonight.

Rejection. Why don't you want me? Why Michelle tonight? What don't I have? What is wrong with me? I feel special, but you don't make me feel special. Why couldn't I leave you? Why couldn't I just let go and find a nice guy who would treat me like a queen? Why did I think so little of myself?

The pain and insecurity felt unbearable, but the thought of leaving felt even more unbearable. My solution was to numb. I became addicted to crystal meth...

I got high at Knott's Berry Farm, and I loved the way it made me NOT feel... NOT care. I didn't feel insecure anymore. I wasn't wondering where you were or how you felt about me. I felt free!

⚘⚘⚘⚘

It was love (or infatuation) at first sight, and I was convinced we were meant to be. I was determined and committed to the outcome I wanted: to be his girlfriend.

I became his girlfriend eventually, and I also experienced a load of pain and shame in that relationship. I wasn't willing to see the truth, and I wasn't willing to let go of him to honor myself. I was too afraid to let him go. My feelings were so intense, I couldn't imagine feeling that way for anyone else.

"When connection to others causes us to disconnect from our true soul self, this is a form of self-abandonment and co-dependency. When connection to others enhances our connection to our true soul self, this is authenticity and inter-dependency."

—Amber Susa

৵৵৵৵

Growing up, I felt different. I never felt like people fully knew me; I always felt slightly disconnected, guarded. Except for when I was on stage.

I grew up going on auditions, filming—away from "normal life." Anytime I allowed my soul to be expressed, I did stand out from the crowd, and I did seem to lose the sense of connection and belonging I craved.

I was the girl who got the lead two years in a row! *Aaaah*, the audacity of the director to cast the same girl two years in a row! People don't like when you stand out. They don't trust that they have their own unique light to shine, so they certainly don't want your light to shine. It threatens their beliefs, their stories.

I betrayed myself and became whom I thought people wanted me to be. And I felt alone a lot. I was in this loop of searching for belonging and betraying myself.

This pattern continued throughout my life, and I was completely unaware. This is how the subconscious works. A belief is born, unbeknownst to us, that creates a pattern. We think we're making choices, but really, we're just on autopilot, returning to our default settings.

We just think we're unlucky in love, choosing the "wrong people." But really, we're "choosing" from a belief about who we are and what we deserve.

I believe there is a paradigm shift occurring, and our consciousness is changing; our systems are changing, and the way we see the world is changing. The way of existing in the energy of tribal survival is shifting.

Connection through "tribe" is still very important, because we're wired to be in community, which can be a beautiful thing. But the order of things, the priorities, are flipping.

Many of us have been existing in a more codependent dynamic, where belonging to community was the priority, and belonging to ourselves was secondary. Now, we are emerging into a new way of being, where belonging to ourselves is becoming the priority, and our connection with community is born from this place of alignment with our true selves.

We Are Loyal to the Beliefs in our Family Systems

Years ago, when my kids were very young, we lived in a condo in Redondo Beach. It was a wonderful place to live, but I longed for a yard where my kids and I could go outside and play.

My husband was often gone on the weekends, working, and I was home with the little ones. It felt overwhelming to take them places by myself, but it felt claustrophobic staying indoors all weekend. I thought moving to a house with a yard was the solution.

The homes in our neighborhood were expensive, and my mom often mentioned how absurdly high-priced it was to live there. Why not move to Long Beach, where they lived and it was more affordable, so we could be closer? We only lived about thirty-five minutes away, but it wasn't down the street, like my sister and her family.

I played out the scenarios, and at times, it felt like a really good solution. But in my heart, moving back to Long Beach, where I grew up, didn't feel like it was my destiny. I felt guilty. If Long Beach was good enough for my family, wasn't it good enough for me?

I have learned a lot about the subconscious beliefs that are passed down and the loyalty we hold for these beliefs in our family systems. Beliefs about money, how we spend it, and what wealth means are often riddled with complexity and guilt.

Can't I love them and still follow my heart? Can't I honor and appreciate every choice they've made, and at the same time feel okay to choose my own path? "Isn't Long Beach good enough for you?" This is the subtext I could imagine hearing under my mom's comments and practical reasons for why Long Beach was the right choice, the smart choice, the safe choice.

I loved my childhood, I loved where I grew up, and I wouldn't change a thing. I am not too good for anything. It's just that Long Beach was chosen for me, when my parents were finding their way, finding what made sense for them. Now that I am deciding to be a grownup and make choices as a grownup (not seeking approval or asking for someone else to give me the answer), then it is fair that, as I find my own way, I make choices that feel right for me.

It can be so uncomfortable, making these choices, especially when you've been accustomed to needing everyone's agreement and approval.

☙☙☙☙

Chapter 3

The Weight of Carrying Someone Else's Pain

"Empaths feel more deeply, more intensely, and more persistently than those around us. We even feel what other people are afraid to feel within themselves."
—Mateo Sol, author, *Awakened Empath*

Perhaps my empathic nature caused me to feel my pain and the pain of others more deeply. Perhaps I took on the pain that my family members had experienced but had suppressed, because of my deep sensitivity.

We maintained the "perfect family" image, but clearly there was pain, there was trauma, and there were unhealed wounds. Maybe my little empath self could sense this. Maybe this informed the role I would assume in my family and in relationships moving forward.

Being Sensitive Is Not A Compliment

I remember the first time I read an article about highly sensitive and empathic children. I was floored! What someone else might have brushed off felt like the end of the world to me. And it made me feel shame, like something was wrong with me for feeling this way.

Perhaps this was why I always felt so different, why I felt like I was playing a different game than everyone else and felt so ill-equipped.

"That annoying sound is probably significantly more annoying to a highly sensitive person. While it's hard to say anyone is a fan of annoying noises, highly sensitive people are, on a whole, more, well, sensitive to chaos and noise. That's because they tend to be more easily overwhelmed and overstimulated by too much activity."
—Elaine Aron, *The Highly Sensitive Person*

I Feel Different

Sometimes, it feels like I've come here to Earth to play a certain game, and I know the rules and feel confident in my abilities. But when I arrive on Earth, there has been a mistake, and the game I have prepared for is not the game everyone else is playing. And I don't know the rules for this new game. I only know the rules for the game I was prepared to play.

My strategy is to be love. When I arrive here on Earth, that strategy appears to be obsolete. I feel naïve and unprepared. I feel different. I do not have the rule-book for the game these humans are playing. I try desperately to learn the new rules, so I can play with them, but they require skills I am not familiar with, skills I do not have.

I try to use my skills, the ones I am wired with, and this seems to cause me pain. In fact, it appears I am losing their game over and over. Sometimes, it feels like I want to go back to wherever it is I came from... It's too hard, too painful, trying to be like these others. It doesn't feel natural.

I do the things they do and try to be like them, because it is lonely otherwise. But their rules don't make sense to me. And my rules don't seem to apply.

In addition to being a highly sensitive empath, I have also discovered, through the system of Human Design, that I am a projector, which only accounts for approximately twenty-percent of the human population. This could also explain why I always felt different... I literally am.

I have found Human Design to be an incredibly validating and comforting modality and would recommend it to anyone wanting to have a better understanding of themselves and those around them.

༺ঌঌঌঌ༻

Journal Entry

My true self is sensitive and kind, deep and passionate, emotional and fierce. I can be a people-pleaser and a codependent. I can dim my light to make other people comfortable.

I was listening to Oprah's new book, The Path Made Clear, *and the part with Glennon Doyle struck me. She talks about the "25 Things About Me" list on Facebook... Her list was deep and true and raw, and other people talked about hummus.*

I can relate... I don't want to talk about fucking hummus... I want to talk about why I'm here, what I've been through, where I'm going; my dreams, my fears, my dark shadow. The intense joy I feel, and the deep shame I experience. Why don't other people want to talk about this? Are they afraid, or do they just not care?

I was at a friend's house the other day… Nice friends, good people, but no desire to go below the surface with me. They were talking about the other couple's marital problems… friends who would be joining us shortly. They wanted to talk about what was wrong with them. And again, another couple later in the afternoon, after they left, we talked about them, too.

I blurted out, "Well, we've been on the verge of divorce for the last couple years!"

It's the truth, and if they are going to talk about my marriage when I leave, I want to have already said the shit they are going to talk about. I'd rather talk about other shit… Why have I been on the verge of a divorce? Why is that husband so terribly insecure and jealous? Why did the other husband leave to come to the party without telling his wife? There is a reason!

I don't want to just sit there and talk about it… I'm curious about why! We all have shit! We all have lessons to learn and reasons why we do the things we do. Those are the conversations I want to have. I don't want to talk about hummus, and I don't want to talk about other people's marital problems, unless they are included in the conversation and the intention is to seek to understand what we can learn and how we can heal.

I get it. I'm different. I've spent much of my life feeling different.

৯৯৯৯

Journal Entry – Early Motherhood

I have always been a lot. A lot of energy. Too much. Too sensitive. Too big of feelings. Too expressive. Too many "unrealistic" dreams. Too much of an optimist. Too naïve. Too needy.

I imagine, as a young child, I was a lot. My daughter is a lot. So much energy. So much zest. So much personality. Big, intense feelings. She is a reflection of me. But she is also her own person.

Growing up, I wonder if my mom felt like I do at times... So in love with me, but overwhelmed with my a lot-ness, my abundance of energy. It can be overwhelming.

I am a raw nerve sometimes. My nervous system feels different than what I see in others. I feel like my nervous system is so vulnerable and raw to energy. I am a highly sensitive empath. I feel like I'm on sensory overload sometimes, if there is too much going on, too much noise, too much clutter, too much mess.

My parents started me in dance class at a young age, then on to gymnastics, then back to dance. I was at an activity every night of the week, as I remember it. Perhaps it was clear I needed an outlet for my too much-ness. I wonder if it was hard for my mom, if she felt a sensory overload with my energy. I wonder if I could sense that?

Since becoming a mother, my sensitive nervous system has become even more obvious. The noise and chaos and clutter... the people needing me, talking to me, touching me. I love them so dearly, it makes me cry, and it also makes me cry for the guilt I feel about having negative feelings about them, that at times all I want is to be alone. I resist that feeling, because I'm not in the moment.

I think of the future, of times they won't want me, and I have shame and remorse for time wasted, not wanting to be with them. I numb my nervous system. On Sundays, I'm home with them often all day. It feels too much to take them anywhere... too much.... Too overwhelming... too stressful. When I take them to the park, I often regret it, worrying about them, tense in my body, not relaxed, stressed. So, I opt to stay home.

I'm bored, I drink to numb my nervous system. I drink to make the day feel more fun and adventurous. I drink to give myself permission to unplug, go off-grid, so I don't have to feel my too-muchness. It's a cycle I am ready to release. It makes me feel shame. It keeps me stuck in the old stories. I am ready to release the old stories.

I desire to simply let my daughter be herself, her too-much energy. She sings the books she's supposed to read for homework. She's been dancing more, singing more. I see more in her wanting to be expressed. I want to embrace this. I want to embrace the more that is wanting to be expressed in me.

I feel burdened by activities that don't bring me joy. I just want to do what I'm great at, what I love. I have a story that tells me that's not reality. That is not life. You don't just get to do the things you love. Sometimes, you have to do things you don't like. That is called life, being responsible. Realistic, practical.

I dream about spending my days filled with just the things I love... teaching, dancing, performing, playing, creating, collaborating, being in solitude, enjoying my *family. Right now, I'm out of balance. I need more of what I love, my bliss, my purpose.*

Maybe I'm drinking as a way to "balance" and add more "play"? But it's not doing what needs to be done. It's not creating more balance. In fact, it's creating less balance, because the creative energy that so desperately wants to flow and be expressed gets quiet, when I lower my frequency with these self-sabotaging habits. I move back into a place of fear. I do not trust the Universe is guiding me and supporting me.

∽∽∽∽

I wrote this before I understood how the accumulation of stress and tension works. I had guilt and shame for the part of me that struggled to feel patient and calm with my young children. I compared myself to an ideal version of the "new mom" I thought I was supposed to be. I didn't understand that, because of my lifetime accumulated stress, the subconscious beliefs I held, and the emotions that were repressed or suppressed, I didn't have the expanded capacity to hold space in the way I do today.

I would later be introduced to my friend, teacher, and healer, Christopher Lee Maher, author of *Free for Life: A Navy Seal's Path to Inner Freedom and Outer Peace*, and founder of True Body Intelligence. His work focuses on reducing lifetime accumulated stress and tension in the body.

My work with him in February 2020 has been profoundly impactful in the way I am able to show up as a woman and a mother. Back then, I didn't have the tools I have now or know how to communicate from a place of empowerment. I was in the energy of proving and unworthiness. I have such compassion for the version of me that was doing her best back then.

ৰ৳৳৳

Journal Entry 2015 - Running on Empty

How do you know when your tank is running low? Are you in-tune with your body? With your feelings and emotions? With your reactions and responses?

As I continue to practice mindfulness and allow myself to get quiet and listen, I become more in touch with my needs and when I'm running on empty. You know, those moments when you thought you were feeling fine, and then, all of a sudden, you start to get annoyed about little, insignificant things, lose your patience and-become anxious.

Many of us are unaware and simply react, blaming others and lashing out without examining what is really going on and making it a priority to fill our tanks. Do you know what kind of gas your car needs?

The overwhelm of day-to-day tasks can be depleting, and if we don't pay attention and fill our tanks before we completely run out of gas and become raving you-know-whats, we end up spending more time than we want feeling frustrated, stressed out, angry, and exhausted. I am learning to see the signs, listen to the messages, and act.

For example, the other night, after I put my one-year-old son down to bed, I could feel the pangs of depletion and overwhelm.... Before I yelled at my three-year old or got into a fight with my husband, I asked for what I needed. I asked my husband to watch our daughter while I took a bath.

In the past, I would have pushed through and been triggered by the frustrating bedtime rituals and routine. Instead, I filled up my tank in a nice warm Epsom-salt bubble bath and read some of my book. It's truly remarkable how a little self-care goes a long way.

When I came downstairs, I was recharged and better able to handle the tantrum that preceded bedtime. I was patient and calm; I allowed my daughter to have her feelings without being triggered and escalating the emotion of the moment. I touched her leg and waited for the feelings to pass. Funny thing about feelings... They always pass... And they seem to pass more quickly when met with calm patient empathy.

This is a quality of the True Divine Feminine: holding space – being love. I went to bed that night exhausted from the day but with no regret for my behavior, no guilt or shame for my reactions.

Getting quiet, getting connected to myself and my feelings, and listening to the messages... I am a work in progress, but the more I recognize the need for self-care and act before it's too late, the better I feel, the more connected I am in my relationships, and the more peace I have.

It is not selfish to take care of myself. It is quite the opposite, it is selfish to ignore my empty tank and mindlessly react to the people and circumstances in my life.

❦❦❦❦

Journal Entry - Early in my Healing Journey

I just discovered the book, The Highly Sensitive Person: How To Thrive When The World Overwhelms You *by Dr. Elaine Aron. I just took her quiz, "Are you a highly sensitive person?" It all makes sense now! Holy shit! I am a highly sensitive person!*

Now, if you ask people in my life, they would respond with an emphatic, "Duh!" Yes, I've always known I was sensitive, but it wasn't until I read this article that I fully grasped what that meant and why, for my entire life, I've felt different...

I feel more deeply, I am more animated and expressive, I am loud and big, and I am more easily overwhelmed by situations that others seem to breeze through without a hitch. I react more emotionally than others... Things BOTHER me!

Why can't I just be a "go with the flow" kind of person? Why do I take things so personally? Why do situations that seem to cause other people zero stress cause me tremendous amounts of stress?

"Snap out of it," "Toughen up," "Get over it," and, "Don't take it so personally..." Triggering comments I've tried to refute but, deep down, feel shame for not being able to. I couldn't seem to muster the strength to get over things that caused me turmoil. I couldn't seem to let go of people's comments that hurt my feelings or offended me... or caused me to doubt myself. I played things over and over in my head.

I never thought I was an angry person. In fact, I've prided myself on being an optimistic and positive person, always seeing the good and the bright side of things. And yet, I'm angry! I've discovered, I'm angry...

I'm angry that I'm so easily thrown by people and situations into a state of stress and anxiety. That I so easily give my power away to others, making them the dictators of my feelings. Imagine if I were able to process my feelings more successfully and not feel so defensive.

❦❦❦❦

I remember writing this; I remember feeling this way. And although there are still times when I temporarily give my power away, I have come so far. I have grown so much.

I am so incredibly grateful for the healing journey I am on, the journey that has led me back to my most empowered self. Today, I am able to process my feelings successfully most of the time, and when I falter, I have the tools that bring me back to my center. Today, I have a deeper understanding of what triggers me and an appreciation for my sensitivity. Most of the time, I see it as the gift it is and the not curse that I felt it was for so long.

Today, I have a better understanding of why early motherhood felt so challenging. I didn't have the tools. I didn't know how to regulate my nervous system. I felt like I was supposed to be able to handle it all and felt awful about myself when I couldn't.

Today, I am more in tune with my body and can feel when I am needing to regulate and calm. Sometimes, all it takes is a few minutes outside, breathing, listening to a guided meditation. And I also recognize that, when kids are really young, there isn't always the opportunity available to take a time-out, in which case giving ourselves grace and compassion for where we are in the moment can be incredibly effective and healing.

❦❦❦❦

Journal Entry - Early Motherhood

Since having kids, I have been accused of being uptight. I feel angry and defensive at this accusation, but the problem is, it appears to be true. I had no idea how uptight I was! Did kids make me uptight? Or was I uptight all along and didn't even know it?

Today, I was so proud of myself. We did art in the backyard. I know... What the heck is there to be proud of about doing art with your kids in the backyard? So sad, how critical I am of myself. I have no room for myself to be imperfect and messy, so how can I allow my children to be imperfect and messy? It was incredibly triggering!

This art involved finger paint and mess and paint all over clothes and faces and arms and legs and the back fence. I'm trying to let go, to be easier going, to allow my kids to be kids and learn from their wild and creative imaginations. I'm trying to learn from them and relish how their beautifully innocent brains work.

I did it. There was paint everywhere, and then, just as I was ready to get everyone cleaned up, my daughter insisted she use her Play-Doh in her art project. I hate Play-Doh. Who loves Play-Doh? It is so messy!

I have a thing about messy... I'm still trying to figure that out. Perhaps it's a control thing, but I really prefer things to not be messy... I like clean and tidy. You can imagine how having a two- and a four-year-old really puts a wrinkle in my need to by tidy.

Anyhow, I was feeling pretty liberated and proud, so I said, "What the heck, let's do Play-Doh! Sure honey, here's your Play-Doh... All of it! Have at it. Make the biggest mess you can possibly make... I'm okay with it!"

I am changing. I am growing and evolving into a go-with-the-flow kind of mom. It's like I'm fighting with another part of myself as I watch them make a mess. One part of my brain is cringing at the painted handprints on the fence, while the other part of my brain is saying, "Yes! Be creative, be free. Yes... This is good. This is fun!"

Oh yes, you want me to fill up the bucket with water, so you can splash it all about and walk in it and step into the bucket? Why do I hesitate? What do I not love about this? I'm uptight... I'm fucking uptight, but it's okay, because, in the moment, I actually feel like I'm becoming less uptight.

So, it's time to get cleaned up and take a bath. I struggle with bathtime. But I'm hopeful things are going so well, perhaps bath time will be as liberating tonight as the rest of today's activities have been. In fact, it is...

Oh wow, I'm really proud of myself! I am doing so well... I am not being uptight. I am being free and fun and loving my children!

Bath time goes well, we get dressed and downstairs to watch a movie! Oh, I'm so excited... My goal of having a smooth, happy afternoon into the evening is happening. There's no way things can go wrong... I feel strong and calm and happy!

And then... I put on the movie we started watching this morning before school, and I'm trying to find where we left off. Oh yes, we're all on the same page—my two-year-old son and my almost four-year-old daughter, we're all on the same page, excited to watch Tangled *for the tenth time!*

I'm fast-forwarding, and my daughter starts to scream and cry. Oh, fuck! Really? Things were going so well... I did such a good job.... Didn't that count for something? Doesn't that mean we're not going to have any problems tonight?

Her mere frustrated cry escalates into a full-blown screaming, kicking freak out!

My daughter has big feelings. Yes, I know what you're thinking.... So do I... Yes, it's true, my daughter has big intense feelings, just like me. And here we are. I am so quickly transported into a frustrated, angry, helpless state.

I try to use compassion... I touch her leg. I tell her I want to help her work through her feelings, identify what the problem is, and communicate without incoherently screaming and crying and kicking her legs in my direction. It doesn't work... And here we are again. It was all for naught... fail! A big Mom Fail.

I feel so fucking frustrated and mad at my almost four-year-old daughter. I loved so intensely and fully just two minutes ago, and now, I find myself feeling rage and frustration. Didn't it count for something, all the fun we just had? How good I was? How well I did at not being uptight?

And now I am in the other room, writing... It is a newfound way of expressing myself... My truth... Without stuffing or needing to say it out loud to my husband, when he gets home. Perhaps purging my emotions here will be enough so that, when he walks into the door, I can be pleasant and not hate him for not having to experience the journey I just took.

I now feel guilty, like I need to go into the living room and watch the movie with my two precious children... I'm *losing precious time with them... Soon, they will be teenagers and want nothing to do with me.*

Oh, that's the crazy thing about motherhood... I can feel such intense aggravation and frustration in one minute and then, the next minute, I want to scoop her up and hold her and cry at my feelings, which I have shame and guilt for having. Oh, the life of a mother!

ఌఌఌఌ

My kids are older now, nine and eleven, and I have done a lot of work to regulate my nervous system and remove stress and tension from my body and my life. I have also adjusted my belief system. I don't believe that one tough moment means I have failed as a mother or that it ruins the rest of the day.

Back then, I had no awareness or understanding of the reason I felt so ill-equipped and struggled to control the circumstances to feel okay. My nervous system couldn't handle it. I also didn't have acceptance for the fluctuation in my own emotions and brought my shame into the experience of motherhood.

Thankfully, today, most of the time, when my children are having big feelings, I am much less triggered, and I have a greater capacity to hold space, because my nervous system is regulated the majority of the time through consistently using all the tools in my toolkit.

ఌఌఌఌ

Journal Entry 2015

Becoming a mother three and a half years ago has been my greatest aha... It has truly pushed me to "uncover, discover and discard" all that stands in my way of feeling perfect, whole, and complete.

I feel a calling to teach others, to share and inspire others to do the work I have been doing. I want to be authentic. For the first time in a long time, I have a certainty that the work I'm doing is where I belong and is what will heal me. I want to be at peace; I want to truly love and accept myself, so I can love and accept others.

I want to have a deep, spiritual connection with all the people in my life, especially my family. I want to raise my children with these principles and practices. I want to feel like I am truly living my fully-expressed purpose. I have many moments of feeling empowered and successful... and I want to keep peeling the onion.

∽∽∽∽

The Pain of Self-Abandonment

I went to drug rehab for crystal methamphetamine when I was nineteen years old. People who knew me were shocked! It didn't fit the image... perfect family, perfect girl, dancer, gymnast, straight-A student; bubbly, energetic, optimistic.

This is who I had always been. This is who I was when I met my first love, Brown Bronco, at the age of fifteen. I was naïve. My heart was open and pure. And just like I felt things deeply, I also loved deeply. And I fell hard for this beautiful, blond boy. A young boy being raised by a single mother, whose dad had moved to another state and didn't seem to make much effort to see him and his brother.

God only knows the wounds and subconscious beliefs that were born for him at a young age. I know the wounds my own mom suffered, not being cherished by her father the way every child hopes to be. And so, I can imagine the kinds of wounds my beautiful, blond boy suffered. And this is who I fell in love with.

And somewhere deep inside me, a role had already been established, a role as a fixer and saver, a holder of other people's pain... Trying to save them from their pain and to help them carry the weight of some of it with my love, my pure heart.

I had no idea how this beautiful, blond boy's wounds would affect me, and I took it all so very personally. His rejection, his cheating—it all felt very personal. He was rejecting me; he was cheating on me. And therefore, something must be wrong with me.

There were moments when I felt so special, when he would open his heart to me, only to close it again, becoming stoic and unavailable once more. The roller coaster was painful and yet addictive. I couldn't leave. And I gave my power away time and time again, until there was nothing left.

Once it was gone, I didn't know how to get it back. But I found ways that made me feel like I was getting it back, coping strategies like drinking alcohol and smoking pot. It temporarily eased the intensity of caring too fucking much, along with the pain of all the self-abandonment and betrayal.

When I met Brown Bronco, the only alcohol I had tasted was the residue on the ice cubes from my parents' occasional after-dinner Kahlua. And I was adamant that I would never ever take drugs! But coping strategies are born out of desperation, and they work until they don't.

It was gradual... a wine cooler here, a Coor's Light there, a bong toke, a joint... All the other teenagers were doing it, and I wanted so badly to belong, it became easier and easier to say yes to all kinds of things I swore I'd never say yes to.

When I was introduced to crystal meth, drinking alcohol and smoking pot had become normalized, so introducing something like meth felt less shocking than it would have, years prior. It was New Year's Eve, and a group of us were pre-partying at Brown Bronco's house before leaving for the larger festivities.

A friend of mine led a group of us girls into the bathroom and pulled out a Ziplock bag with yellowish-white powder and a rolled-up dollar bill. It was a special occasion, she said. This was apparently something she had been doing for a while unbeknownst to me.

All the other girls were in, so, without thinking too much about it, I took the rolled-up dollar bill and snorted the laid-out line like I'd seen the other girls do. I felt an instant jolt! My nose burned, and my eyes watered. An awful, bitter liquid dripped down into my throat, and I guzzled the beer I was drinking to wash it down.

Almost immediately, I felt superhuman. A wave of confidence rushed over me. I didn't give a fuck... and I absolutely loved that!

For the rest of that night, I carried this newfound freedom with me, not worrying about where Brown Bronco was or who he was talking to. It helped me not care in a way that felt so empowering and had been unattainable before.

And I wasn't about to let go of this strategy and solution… It felt like my only hope at the time.

I quickly became addicted, adopting a daily habit. I lost twenty pounds that I didn't need to lose, dropped out of college, pulled away from my family, and became a shell of a human being.

Sometimes, our coping strategies become our greatest demise. My parents confronted me many times, and each time, I lied and accused them of being nosy and annoying. Couldn't they remember being a teenager? I was nasty and convincing… My acting skills paid off… or did they?

I absolutely hated myself for lying to them… We had always been so close. But I couldn't bring myself to tell them the truth, until one morning. At that point, I was nineteen years old. My parents were losing control, and I had already lost control. My once compliant and respectful nature had gone out the window, and I was spiraling down further and further away from my true soul self. This drug, which had once made me feel empowered and invincible, had turned against me and was stealing the very essence of my soul. I wanted to stop, but I could not.

One night, I went out with my friends to some party and ended up passing out at my best friend's house, without calling my parents to tell them I wasn't coming home that night. This was the only promise I had still been able to keep… At the very least, I would let them know if I wasn't coming home. But this particular night, I didn't call them, didn't let them know.

I drove home the next morning after everyone had left and crawled into my bed to sleep off the intense fatigue and withdrawal I was experiencing. My mom had gone into work and called the friends she had phone numbers for, to find out where I was. Having no luck, she'd decided to go home and get her phone book to make some more calls.

She walked in the door and found me in my bed, passed out, wearing nothing but my underwear... skin and bones, shockingly pale, dark circles under my eyes, with mascara streaming down my face. It pains me to imagine the image my mom had to encounter.

Once again, she confronted me, and instead of lying, like I had every other time, I told the truth. I don't know why this was the moment I was able to tell the truth, but I did, and I am forever grateful.

"Mom, I have a drug problem. Please help me," I sobbed, feeling equal parts shame and relief. My secret was out, and the distance my drug addiction had created between me and my family instantly vanished.

I collapsed into my mom's arms as she hugged me tightly. At that moment, I knew I was safe. She never once shamed me or blamed me. She held me like a small child, and even though she didn't know if everything was going to be okay, in that moment, she made me feel like it was.

That's the gift of a mother... a superhuman, supernatural, Divine Love that provides comfort like nothing else, if you're lucky. Many years later, I would experience the birth of this superhuman, supernatural, Divine Love in myself, when my daughter, Dawson, was born. It felt brand-new and intensely familiar all at the same time.

This moment when I confessed my shameful secret to my mom still brings me to tears all these years later, imagining the gut-wrenching terror she must have felt, the thought of losing her daughter. Her brother, my Uncle Jeff, had been a drug addict, and he wasn't okay; he didn't make it through. I cannot fathom having to go through this with my own daughter.

Please God, let my healing, my remembering, be enough for her to never abandon herself the way I have. May she see me living my truth and loving myself... May I be an example to her. May I empower her and inspire her to always live her truth and to love herself above all else.

My mom was my rock; she held it together until she got into her car after dropping me off at rehab and then fell apart. She was grateful to have an answer for my behavior and to have found a place where I could start my recovery. But she was terrified I would end up like her brother, the sensitive, sweet soul who became a heroin addict and took his own life at the age of twenty-six.

I've often wondered why did I get to recover and why didn't he? I don't have the answer, but I do know, in my darkest moments, he was my guardian angel, encouraging me to be honest and ask for help. Thank you, my sweet Uncle Jeff, for being my angel.

After I got out of my twenty-eight-day rehab, I got sober and became the "perfect girl in recovery." I went to 12-Step meetings every day, got a sponsor, worked the steps, and started sponsoring other girls. I did everything they told me and followed the program to a T.

I was so unbelievably grateful to reconnect with the part of me that is joyful and hopeful and full of life... The girl who lives in awe and wonder. I have always had a belief and faith in all things spiritual; the mystical and magical have always deeply resonated. I think that's why I loved AA for so long... It reconnected me with the God of my understanding and gave meaning to things in life that didn't always make sense. And I finally felt the sense of belonging I had always been searching for.

For the first eleven years of my sobriety, it was in those rooms where I found my purpose and place in life. I met my first husband when I was two years sober, at the age of twenty-one. When we met, I had completely disconnected from my creative self and was solely focused on my recovery. After we got married, I decided to take some classes at a local community college, as I had dropped out before getting sober.

In addition to the academic classes I enrolled in, I decided to take a dance class. No matter how many times I have walked away, my soul always calls me back to creative expression. That dance class at Citrus Community College with my wonderful teacher, Diane, woke something up inside of me that had been asleep. I felt more alive than I had in years. That's when you know you are coming into alignment with your true soul self: you feel alive, you feel the most like you. And dancing has always been something that has made me feel the most like me.

And, of course, there is acting. As soon as I started dancing again, I felt this desire rise up inside me to start acting again, calling me back. I couldn't ignore it.

I talked to my husband about it, and he encouraged me to follow my heart. When we met, I was sober and working as a receptionist at BFI Medical Waste in Vernon, California. To say I wasn't fully embodying all of me is an understatement; but it's an important part of my journey, and without contrast showing us what we don't want, we can't know what we do want.

I started researching acting classes and found my way to the Beverly Hills Playhouse. The Playhouse was doing a showcase, and two of my scenes from class were chosen. I was elated! I felt like me, the me I was born to be: a bright shining light on stage, expressing all of me. I felt at home, like I was made to be there.

The more I reconnected with the parts of me that I had drifted away from, the less I felt connected to my husband and to the people in the 12-Step rooms. I was beginning to feel even more like myself, my authentic soul self, whom I had abandoned, and it felt so good. And it felt scary.

As we grow and change, we either grow and change with the people in our lives or we don't. We've all heard the saying, "People come into your life for a reason, season, or a lifetime." In my case, my first husband and I came together for a reason and a season, but not a lifetime.

It was one of the hardest decisions I've ever made, but I left that marriage. Not because there was anything wrong with him... He was and is a wonderful guy. I just knew in my heart there was more for me.

๑๑๑๑

Born To Fly

She was born with wings... Born to fly. Those who are meant to fly, those who are born with wings, are not meant to stay in one place for long. Have you ever seen a butterfly stay in one place? Or a hummingbird? No... They come to visit, share their beauty, bring their magic, and then they fly off to share their magic with someone else.

She was made to feel broken for wanting to fly. She tried to live a life as though she didn't have wings... But she kept bumping into things... Her soul longed to soar, but she kept trying to ignore.

The pain of leaving people and situations... Was it truly her pain? Or the pain of the people she was leaving that had her pause, doubt, cry?

Always wanting more... searching and seeking... moving from one to the next... Another project, another man, another possibility. Nobody wanted to fly with her... They all wanted her to stay on the ground with them and be satisfied...

But she had wings. Staying on the ground with wings felt so heavy... She was meant to use them.

She left two marriages... She left a perfectly good business... She doesn't have life-long friends...

They say she's a failure because she flew away... But isn't that what she was born to do?

She never meant to hurt anyone... She tried to stay, but she had to go. She can still love you and fly away. In fact, she'll love you more, if you tell her to soar.

⋞⋟⋞⋟

Why do I feel shame for wanting *more*? I shouldn't! I should feel empowered to make choices that feel right... that feel good... that make me happy... that allow me to live a life where I am the *most me... All of me*!

This is my journey... I owe it to my soul to follow the whispers of my heart... to fulfill my destiny and model to my children what it is to live an inspired life! Yes, the answers are inside of me. I just need to get quiet and listen.

How Patterns Are Born

When my mom was a young girl, her family moved a lot. She attended a new school every year, growing up, and always felt like the outcast. She never felt like she belonged or was accepted.

Her father always had a new opportunity or business venture, so, without considering the effects this constant uprooting would have on the rest of the family, he announced the move and off they would go. Over the years, my mom has shared her painful memories of always being the new girl in class and her deep insecurities, which were born from the rejection and lack of belonging she experienced.

According to Vienna Pharaon, in her book, *The Origins of You*, there are five origin wounds: worthiness, belonging, trust, safety, and prioritization. I am certain that my mom has some, if not all of these wounds, from her childhood. I am also certain it is human nature to try to correct these wounds, whether consciously or not, when we start to have families of our own.

My mom did her very best to make sure I felt prioritized and secure growing up… to be spared the pain she'd experienced as a young girl with a father who didn't prioritize her. And in my own little way, I assumed the role of the healer at a very young age and did my best to make sure my mom felt safe and loved.

On some subconscious level, I believe I intuitively felt her buried and hidden pain, and I began a pattern of wanting to save people from their pain, codependent patterns I would repeat throughout my life.

My dad had his own inner child wounds as well, having lost his mother to breast cancer when he was only seven. If you ask him about his childhood, he will proudly share how his loving father worked graveyard shifts to support the family, and that he has a tremendous amount of love and respect for the way his dad was able to show up for him and his siblings, despite having lost his beloved wife and having no one with whom to share the responsibilities of raising a family. But despite what a wonderful job my grandpa did, the facts are the facts, and my dad grew up without the love of a mother.

This pattern of me wanting to save people from their pain played out in my life for decades. I would seek out friends and boyfriends who also had buried and hidden pain; my little empathic, sensitive self wanted so much to help people heal and feel loved. I thought my love could save them. What I didn't realize at the time was that, when I volunteered to help carry some of their pain, I often took it on as my own, and the lines became blurred.

The weight of carrying someone else's pain can become great. It was confusing, and I didn't understand why I seemed to feel such deep and intense emotions that didn't stem from anything I could pinpoint in my life. These are all discoveries I have made on my healing journey, trying to make sense of it all; about the generational trauma, subconscious beliefs, and roles I took on in my early years. And what has become clear is that a pattern of codependency was born early on that would, for many years, keep me from flying away and soaring in the way I was born to.

I truly had a wonderful childhood. I grew up feeling loved and supported. I didn't experience any major trauma, except for the by-products of my own self-abandonment, which never made sense to me, given my "perfect" childhood. It wasn't a painful childhood that prompted my quest to understand my own wounds. It was my confusion around the how and why I ended up where I did.

I had so much shame, because I didn't have anyone or anything to blame for my perceived failures. A dark night of the soul in 2014, after the birth of my son, catapulted me onto this healing journey, a journey that has been filled with a desperation to understand how a girl who had everything going for her, a girl who was born with what appeared to be cards stacked in her favor, a bright light filled with awe and wonder, with parents who have enjoyed a loving marriage for over fifty years... could end up a self-abandoning drug-addict, college dropout, and two-time divorcee.

This quest to understand has driven me to delve into and dissect how generational trauma, unhealed wounds, and addiction can get passed down, and how this may have informed the disempowering choices I've made, including the repeated abandonment of my true soul self. It now makes sense to me how the wounds of my parents and their parents and so on have played out in my life. And how it is now my opportunity and obligation to heal these patterns and wounds, so my children might enjoy a more soul-aligned, less self-abandoning life.

I have been accused of overanalyzing and "talking things to death." But I have come to understand that it is this relentless need to understand that took me down the path of investigating the ins and outs of my story.

My search began in 2014, and I am still having regular aha moments. One of those moments happened recently, when I was listening to Vienna Pharaon, author of *The Origins of You*, talk about the prioritization wound.

Interestingly, this particular wound was the one I identified with the least. My parents had always made me their top priority. And then it dawned on me: my *mom* had the prioritization wound; she never felt special enough to earn the attention from her father, forever trying to win his love and matter in his life.

And then I realized that my first boyfriend, Brown Bronco, also had this wound. After his parents' divorce, his father moved to another state and didn't make much effort to maintain a connection; it didn't appear to be a priority. And my childhood best friend... After her parents' divorce, she, too, often felt of secondary importance to her father.

And in many of my adult relationships, looking back, I can see there was a prioritization wound at play. Wow! Lightbulb moment! It makes sense... I see the thread. It wasn't because I was broken or flawed. It was because a pattern was established and a role was assumed. And these roles make us feel safe and needed.

This goes back to the tribal survival concepts... Everyone had a job, and to stray from that job or leave the pack could mean death. And although most of the time there is no threat of actual death in our family dynamics, subconsciously, the threat can feel that severe.

What I also came to understand was that, in her unconscious attempt to heal her own prioritization wound, my mom made me her number-one priority. And I became the reason she mattered... Why she was special and worthy. And while I am quite aware that being someone's priority can be a beautiful gift, I am also aware it can be a huge responsibility.

Where codependence comes into play is the need to uphold that role and responsibility, even to the detriment of one's own well-being. It had always felt random and confusing that I continued choosing relationships that were codependent and sometimes toxic, especially because my role model for relationships is my parents, who have been happily together since the ages of sixteen and seventeen.

Why the hell was I so screwed up? Why did I keep making "bad" choices? Why did I constantly abandon myself to maintain relationships that weren't serving me?

When confronted with these questions, the obvious answer was certainly not, "Well it's because my parents made me too much of a priority... They just loved me too damn much." Nope... In fact, that felt ridiculous and embarrassing. Other people had it much worse... I couldn't possibly claim that as my excuse for being a loser and failure.

And yet, the more time I've spent investigating and excavating, the more it makes sense and brings me a sense of peace. I experienced the other side of the prioritization wound: the pressure of being responsible for someone else's happiness and significance. And what I've come to know deeply is that I am not responsible for anyone's happiness... I am only responsible for my own. And this knowledge brings me a tremendous amount of freedom.

In no way do I blame my mom or dad. I can clearly see how these patterns and wounds have been passed down through so many generations. The codependency and self-abandonment, the dimming of one's own light to make someone else feel special, the unconscious attempts to heal and overcompensate.

I love my family deeply and am so very grateful for the tremendous love and appreciation we have for one another. And I am deeply grateful that my healing journey has brought much healing to my entire family. This work has gifted me such clarity and compassion and has had quite a ripple effect on those I love so dearly.

∽∽∽∽

One recent afternoon, as I was reminiscing about everything I have come to understand, I felt an overwhelming love and appreciation for my mom and was compelled to write her a letter.

April 1, 2023

Dear Mom,

It is because of you that I am able to be the mother I am. Your pure love, your pure heart. I think of the video from my fortieth birthday, when you were interviewed about being my mom, and I can see your sweet face. Your hands cheered as you told me through your tears, "You're so amazing." This image, this message, your voice, your face... etched in my memory forever.

And you have loved me my whole life, through those eyes of amazement... You have been my greatest cheerleader... Even though you never had a cheerleader of your own. My heart aches for the pain you felt as a young girl, moving around year after year, never feeling a sense of belonging, never having a mother or father look at you with this sense of awe and appreciation for who you were... They were too young, too caught up in their own pain, their own wounds.

You are amazing. Despite your wounds, despite never having received that kind of unconditional love and support, you had to become your mother's mother at a young age, never receiving the approval and validation from your wounded father. And yet you were able to give me the love you never felt fully. You are amazing. I grieve your pain as though it was my own. I weep for your wounds and, at the same time, sit in amazement of who you are and what you gave me... a lifetime of cheerleading, a lifetime of unconditional love.

How did you do it? I thought I was breaking the cycles, but you did... You broke the cycles, when you became the mother you never had. And now I get to be a mother to Dawson and Will because of you. Because of your strength, because of your heart, because of your determination and courage.

You are so strong. You've never believed that... I think you've always thought Dad was the strong one... And I'm sad to say, there have been many times in my life I thought that, too. I didn't see your strength as I see it now. And now that I see it, I am amazed.

I carried your wounds with me, I carried Nana's wounds with me... This is who I am... a sensitive soul who feels it all: my own wounds and those of my ancestors. It is my gift, and it has often felt like a curse.

But I am healing, and I am you and you are me... and we are healing. You've always given me a safe place to land... That safety has made all the difference in the world, knowing I am safe, knowing I am loved by you and Dad...

I hope you really know what a great gift you have given me and continue to give me. Today, at Will's game, we were talking about age and death, and I said I can't even go there. I can't even imagine a world where I don't get to pick up the phone and hear your voice... But I know that day will come... hopefully not for a long time.

But I want you to know how amazing I think you are before that day comes… When that day does come, I want to know I've said everything I want to say, nothing left unsaid. I can't say it enough… I want to hug your little girl and shake my fists in the air and tell her how amazing she is, because I know she didn't hear it enough, and she deserved to.

Every little girl deserves to hear how amazing she is from the people who matter the most… Until, one day, she can believe it for herself.

I speak to you woman to woman, and little girl to little girl… I see you and I think you are amazing!

I love you,

Amber Pie

ঙ‍ঙ‍ঙ‍ঙ

The gifts of this work continue to overwhelm me in the best way possible. Below is a letter I received from my eleven-year-old daughter, Dawson, five months after I wrote this letter to my mom. I am in awe of the healing ripple effect and so grateful for the circle of love I am enveloped in.

ঙ‍ঙ‍ঙ‍ঙ

September 28, 2023

Dear Mommy,
You are the most valuable thing in my life. I love you so much. Thank you for caring about me so much. You are the most caring, thoughtful, loving, beautiful person ever! Whenever I see you, I feel safe. I love you so much.

Love,
Dawson

⚜⚜⚜⚜

There is no greater gift than knowing I have a safe place to land and that I am a safe place to land.

Illusions and Stories

During the process of writing this book, I have revisited many of my old journal entries from the past nine years of my healing journey. I came across the entry below, written in 2019, and it blew me away. It's a story that has been on repeat for many years, and one that I am now powerfully rewriting.

As I have shared, a pattern of codependency in relationships was established at an early age. I had zero awareness and understanding of what attracted me to certain relationships. I had no idea there was a thread, an unconscious desire to help others heal by offering to carry the weight of some of their pain; to abandon myself, so I might somehow ease their struggle through my love.

I met my ex-husband on Match.com in 2005, when it was still kind of embarrassing to admit you were online dating.

I had been divorced from my first husband for about a year and was ready to meet someone.

My roommate was on Match.com and encouraged me to sign up. He had one picture on his profile... It was a very cute picture. We connected and talked on the phone for a couple weeks before deciding to meet in person. We hit it off immediately!

I was attracted to him. He was easy to talk to. He made me laugh... a lot. We were both actors. It felt comfortable to be with him, and we fell into a relationship. At the time we met, I had been sober for twelve years and earned the nickname "sober girl" from all his East Coast friends.

Not long into our relationship, he decided to give up acting and pursue other passions and employment. We had joined a theater company together, and although I was really enjoying being back on the stage, doing what I loved, I somehow convinced myself I too was over acting and decided to quit the theater company and take a break from pursuing my passions.

I had just gotten back into alignment with the creative expression my soul longs for, but unconsciously fell into the pattern of choosing a relationship over choosing myself. I thought I had to choose. I didn't realize it was possible to remain in authentic alignment with my soul and be in partnership with someone who had other interests.

At the time, I had no idea the subtle whispers of my subconscious and deep-rooted patterns were guiding and dictating my every decision. And to make matters even worse, in my codependent, self-abandoning nature, I also made the decision to give up my twelve years of sobriety. It felt lonely, being the only sober one, and I really wanted to be in this relationship and not feel so alone.

I gave it a lot of thought, talked to my family about it, and in the end, I decided it was probably just a teenage phase… Besides it was drugs I'd had a problem with, not alcohol.

I gave up acting, I gave up my sobriety, and I became a disempowered version of myself, falling right back into the codependent enmeshment I had experienced in past relationships. I had never established a strong enough sense of myself to truly know who I was, and it became difficult to differentiate what belonged to me and what belonged to him.

Many of the beliefs he held from his conditioned upbringing seeped into my consciousness, and I took on the energy of his limiting beliefs, in addition to my own. His fear became my fear. His wounds became my wounds. The journal entry below is an example of how this played out. It was written one year before I left my marriage.

※※※※

Journal Entry - March 7, 2019

I bought lottery tickets today. I have never bought a Powerball lottery ticket. My mom is always telling me I should go buy one, and I never have.

I need a miracle. I have risked it all to follow my heart and trust the call of my soul. I have sold a business. I have been on the verge of a divorce. I have hives. I am simultaneously stressed and comforted. I don't know why, but I have just trusted that I'll be okay. That I'll be taken care of.

Perhaps, I'm triggered because, deep down, I wonder if I'm just a fool. I wonder if I am all the things I have been accused of—impractical and foolish, an irresponsible, selfish dreamer. I have been accused of making the worst business decision anyone could ever make by leaving my business to follow my heart and listen to my soul. I have been pulled and pushed in this direction. It feels right. It feels good. How can it be wrong?

I just opened Allomi, a sanctuary for holistic health and healing – it is my mission. It feels like an assignment, a calling. How can it be irresponsible and selfish to use my gifts to serve humanity?

God, please send a miracle. I need to make money. I need to contribute financially to my household. I want to prove to him that I made the right decision. I want to keep doing what I'm doing and more. I want to write a book. I want to perform. I want to create a show. I want to heal and help others heal. I want to be a good mom and wife.

I am resentful. I don't want to be resentful, but I am. I have moments where I think I've let go, but in times like this, when I'm driving around in my car, tears streaming down my face, using my nickel to reveal a scratcher that has nothing, typing, crying, praying, begging, breathing, vacillating between certainty and trust and panic...

Come back to the present moment. My life is happening for me, not to me. It's not a game of punishment. That's a tough one for me. A deep-seeded belief that I'm being punished. All the what-ifs, like a tornado, roaring through my mind.

I know, in the spiritual realm, there are limitless possibilities I am not considering. Okay, God, what are some of these possibilities? What if all my crazy dreams weren't crazy? Stories and accusations screaming in my head, causing me to doubt myself.

I want to be an example, an inspiration of following my soul call and having it work out. I want to be an example of miracles. I want financial abundance. I want to be able to take care of my family without this heavy financial fear hanging out constantly. I want to prove to myself and to the world that I'm not crazy for dreaming big, and that "being practical" is not always the answer.

Today, I don't know if an amazing opportunity will present itself and a miracle I've prayed for will happen... Or if we'll need to sell our house and get a divorce in order for me to truly step into my greatness. The energy feels so heavy, so suffocating, so fearful—not me, not mine!

I spent so many years of my life determined to prove to others that I was smart, capable and worthy: worthy of love, worthy of respect. I was desperate for my life to work out, so I could prove to the skeptics and naysayers that I wasn't wrong. I wasn't wrong for wanting more. I wasn't wrong for saying yes to the call of my soul. I wasn't wrong for dreaming big. I wasn't wrong for being me.

Today, I experience a freedom and liberation I never thought possible. Today, I don't need to prove anything to anyone, especially the skeptics and naysayers.

As Brene Brown has so beautifully reminded us in her book, *Daring Greatly*, I am "the man in the area ... striving valiantly ... daring greatly."

I have said yes, and that is something to be proud of. I know who I am. I know why I am here. I trust myself and know my worth. To borrow a line from Brene Brown herself, "If you're not in the arena also getting your ass kicked, I'm not interested in your feedback."

It has become so very clear to me that other people's projections have nothing to do with me. I am only triggered when I am in agreement with the projections, because of past wounds and when I am doubting myself. I am free when I remember the truth, my truth, and there is no better feeling than being free.

✧✧✧✧

Journal Entry - June 2019

Yesterday, I was at a women's empowerment event, and toward the end of the event, the host called me out... She asked for someone to share who hadn't spoken out yet. She said my name.

Thank you, God. I said yes. Vulnerability creates connection. Up until that point, I had been quiet and closed, insecure and shy... My light was out. The question she was asking... "What was our take-away from the event?"

I stood up, holding back my sobs, and told the truth. I told the women I didn't even want to come to the event, because I wasn't where I thought I should be. I told the women I had been at the event the past two years and was passionate and hopeful. But today, I felt ashamed.

Where there is fear, love cannot exist. Fear in the many forms it takes – anger, criticism, judgment, blame. I long for connection, vulnerability, joy, hope, intimacy. Yesterday, at the event, I stood up in front of a full room of ladies and cried. I was vulnerable. I told my truth.

And you know what happened? I felt love. I felt seen and understood. This woman sitting next to me looked me in the eyes with such love and appreciation... She praised me... She told me she loved me. She said I was strong and empowered.

Isn't that funny? I felt the opposite... But she could see me, through my tears of vulnerability. She could still see my strength, even though I felt so weak. I didn't want to go to this event, and I'm so glad I did. I showed up. I said yes.

I sat next to the actress Kim Coles... She literally sat at my table on the chair right next to me, both in the room and at lunch. I've been wanting to create a show... A show about All of Me. A show where art meets transformation. A show that inspires, empowers, educates, and entertains.

Kim Coles is an actress. She helps people tell their story. God put her in the chair next to me. I've been told I don't live in reality. Well, maybe I don't live in your reality! I live in a reality where Kim Coles sits next to me at an event, and after I pour my heart out in front of the room, she puts her hand on my shoulder and says, "You should absolutely do a one-woman show."

Yes, that is the reality I live in!

ৰ্ঠ৽ৰ্ঠ৽ৰ্ঠ৽ৰ্ঠ৽

The amount of energy I have wasted, allowing my limiting beliefs, as well as the limiting beliefs of others, to steal my joy and take me out of the present moment, is immense. All of the worst-case scenarios that never happened... All of the panic and worry... All of the self-doubt and negative self-talk.

I stand here before you, reading this journal entry from years ago, happily divorced, all my needs met, on the other side of the manifestations that were only a seed of desire at the time. They say God works in mysterious ways, and that has absolutely been my experience.

The journal entry above was written in June 2019, and in October 2019, I received a call from a friend whom I hadn't spoken to in years. We had co-created a stage show together back in 2004, just before I met my ex-husband. And she was reaching out to let me know she had written a one-woman show and wanted me to attend the upcoming reading.

After years of not speaking, she'd reached out to me at the exact time I was lining up with the desires of my soul and getting honest about what I truly wanted. She introduced me to Jessica Lynn Johnson, founder of Soaring Solo Artist, the woman who would become the director and producer of my own one-woman show, *Waking Up to All of Me*.

Experiences like this have strengthened my trust muscle, so that, when the voices of self-doubt creep in, the limiting beliefs of my past play on repeat... "You're just a dreamer... You don't live in reality... You're making the worst business decision anyone could ever make..." I have evidence that God hears my prayers and that the desires of my heart are there for a reason. I breathe, I meditate, I pray, I take inspired action, and I trust. And the Universe shows up in miraculous ways.

I wrote and performed the one-woman show I said I'd wanted to create. I wrote this book. I am becoming the woman I was born to be. This is what I know: when someone accuses you of "not living in reality," what they are really saying is, "You don't live in my reality."

This world is filled with many realities... What is true for you is true. For so long, I desperately wanted to prove that I was smart enough, successful enough, capable enough... And what I've realized is that the only person who needs to believe that is me.

When we enter into relationships, we make silent agreements. These are not agreements we have conversations about or are even conscious of. Our actions are the signature on the contract.

At the beginning of my relationship with my ex-husband, I signed on the dotted line with my choices... "I, Amber Susa, hereby agree to give up my twelve years of sobriety and quit acting. I choose this relationship above all else." And this is how our relationship played out.

Because I had never cultivated a strong sense of who I was, separate from the relationship I was in, I had no idea I was abandoning myself. I held a limiting belief that I had to make a choice: be alone and do what I loved to do, or be in a relationship and sacrifice my dreams.

And so, it makes sense that, in 2014, when I had my spiritual awakening and started reconnecting with my true soul self, it caused discord in my marriage. I was remembering the importance of my authenticity and beginning to deconstruct and revise our agreement. I was having a spiritual experience and becoming more of who I am. But to someone who was not having this experience, it appeared I was changing for the worse and being incredibly selfish.

It was devastating to me, because I truly felt I was changing for the better. I was pulling out of the agreement I had made so many years ago, and it was terrifying. How would this new agreement affect us? Affect our marriage?

By choosing to give up my sobriety and quit acting, I'd made an agreement that I would sacrifice myself and prioritize him and our relationship. Self-abandonment and codependency in relationships do not often lead to happy endings, and eventually it all came to a head. A dark night of the soul, followed by a spiritual awakening that would lead me on a journey of returning to my true soul self.

This was the beginning of me listening to the voice of my soul. And the more I listened, the more dissonance grew in my marriage. I had been accustomed to making other people the experts on my life, and here I was, taking back my power and becoming the expert, myself.

Those whom I had given my power away to were not happy with this transformation. And it caused a tremendous amount of fear and anger, and the conflict between us increased.

Fear can show up in very hurtful ways. I felt deeply misunderstood and sad at the growing dissonance. When people are acting from a place of fear, they are not acting from their highest self. And this does not make for a harmonious and supportive relationship.

ॐॐॐॐ

Writing Prompt

What are some of the silent agreements you've made in relationships?

Are those agreements still aligned with who you want to be?

What are some limiting beliefs that keep you stuck?

Are you ready to revise your agreements so they are more aligned with who you were born to be?

Chapter 4

Tired of Living a Lie

In 2014, at the age of forty, I woke up with severe and debilitating low back pain that caused deformity in my torso and a stabbing pain that brought me to my knees.

I was a forty-year-old mother of two children under the age of two, married for the second time, and a co-owner of a successful boutique fitness studio. To all appearances, I had everything a person could want: a perfect family with one girl and one boy, both healthy; a thriving business; a home in a highly desirable beach-town neighborhood; and a full social life.

Where had I gone wrong? What was the problem? Why was my body turning on me? Hadn't I taken good care of it? I worked out all the time, ate healthily. Why was I in such paralyzing pain? Why did I feel so alone and lost?

My body knew the truth. It wasn't perfect. Something was missing. I was missing. I had a breakdown.

I remember sobbing on the floor of my husband's home office, pleading with him to see me, to help me, to love me. And the truth was, it had never been about other people seeing me, loving me, helping me; it was always leading me back to the place where I could see myself, love myself, help myself.

This period of my breakdown included excruciating and paralyzing back pain, a fainting episode, many sobbing nights, therapy appointments, increasing arguments, incredible fear and anxiety, and an overall feeling of drowning and being lost.

I was the co-owner of a popular Pilates and fitness studio, and I couldn't stand up straight, let alone teach a fitness class. I had always been able to rely on my physical body to help me cope, to bring me back to my happy place, to rise above the stresses of life. After my first divorce, I would go to the gym for at least two hours, get on the treadmill, crank up the volume of the music playing in my headphones, and run as fast as I possibly could. That was how I dealt with the stresses of life.

When I was nineteen, struggling with a drug addiction, I would go out dancing to feel free and connect with the sliver of my true self I could still feel, when I danced. And so here I was, with what felt like my world collapsing, and I couldn't run, couldn't dance, couldn't move. I was desperate.

One day, I was having a conversation with my friend, Eden, a fellow fitness expert. I was really struggling and confided in her how, no matter what I did, I couldn't escape the intense pain in my lower back. I had never before experienced that kind of physical pain, and it was really taking a toll on my overall well-being.

Eden had just started a meditation practice, the 21-Day Meditation Experience with Oprah Winfrey and Deepak Chopra, and she suggested I try it. It was all about stress relief and healing, and she thought it could be really helpful.

My only experience with meditation had been in my early twenties, with my first husband, at his AA sponsor's house, and I'd decided right then and there meditation was *not* for me. I'd hated it!

The living room was full of people, seated chair to chair, with a large gong at the front of the room, incense burning and some gentle music playing, as he guided us into the meditation. He asked us to close our eyes, rest our hands gently on our laps, place our feet flat on the ground, and take deep breaths. It was super-weird. I kept opening my eyes, peeking to see if anyone else was as creeped out as I was.

Nope, everyone seemed to be peacefully enjoying themselves, and all I wanted to do was run out of the front door, screaming. It became very clear to me: there are the meditating types, and there are the intense, athletic, go-go-go types. I knew where I belonged, and it wasn't taking deep breaths with a bunch of weirdos.

So, when my friend, Eden recommended that I try this Oprah and Deepak meditation thing, you know I had to be desperate to even consider it. I'll never forget that first night… on my bed, in my room, headphones in. Five minutes felt like fifty. I was antsy and agitated, but my desperation had birthed a willingness and open-mindedness, so I kept going, day after day.

Slowly, over time, I felt less and less restless and more and more at ease. I listened to the words Oprah and Deepak spoke, and they began to resonate and bring me comfort.

☙☙☙☙

Oprah Winfrey & Deepak Chopra
21-Day Meditation Challenge: Perfect Health

Oprah's soothing voice spoke these words:

Welcome, everyone. I am so happy you're joining us for our 21-day meditation challenge, Perfect Health. Over the next twenty-one days, we're going to explore the many ways we can all start to take control of our own health and wellbeing.

So, beginning today, week one, we prepare ourselves for perfect health and gain a greater understanding of what our bodies and minds are capable of. In our second week, we learn techniques that help us invite balance into our lives. And then, in week three, we're going to integrate all of these techniques, so that we can truly begin to live perfect health.

I'll be doing it along with you. So, make yourself comfortable, as Deepak begins to share with us his many years of experience and wisdom in this exciting field of mind body medicine. And then, we'll enjoy our very first meditation together.

I began to feel hope. This concept of "mind-body medicine" felt really good to me. It felt like things were making sense and that everything was happening for a greater purpose.

I was beginning to wake up, reconnect with my true soul self, the me I was born to be. I could hear the whispers of my inner voice, my inner knowing, and it felt incredible and empowering. I had forgotten that she existed. When I had made the agreement to abandon myself, I unknowingly had muted that little voice inside, and I was so happy to discover she hadn't disappeared for good.

A door had been opened, an invitation had been sent, and I was saying *yes*. I have come to learn that these invitations are often sent in the form of painful experiences.... physical pain or illness, a traumatic event, relationship issues, or a tragic loss... and we can either choose to say *yes* to the invitation or be in resistance and say *no*. I am grateful I said yes then, and that I continue to say yes each time a soul invitation presents itself.

Once I said yes, the synchronicities started rolling in, and the Universe began sending more information my way. A book recommendation: *Healing Back Pain: The Mind Body Connection* by Dr. John E. Sarno. This book reinforced what I was beginning to learn in my meditation practice about the mind-body connection and the concept that emotions could affect the physical body.

Sarno introduced the term TMS, tension myositis syndrome, whereby physical pain is a consequence of repressed emotions, particularly anxiety and anger. I had never considered myself an angry person. In fact, I was an optimist, always looking for the good. I could easily see where other people in my life had repressed anger, but not me!

It's always so much easier to see other people's issues... Much harder to look in the mirror and see our own. But as much as I resisted the notion that my repressed anger was responsible for my back pain, so much of what Sarno talked about resonated, and I couldn't help but explore the possibilities of what was hiding beneath the surface:

> *The pain is due to TMS, not to a structural abnormality. The direct reason for the pain is mild oxygen deprivation. TMS is a harmless condition, caused by my repressed emotions. The principal emotion is my repressed anger.*
>
> *TMS exists only to distract my attention from the emotions. Since my back is basically normal, there is nothing to fear. Therefore, physical activity is not dangerous. And I must resume all normal physical activity.*
>
> *I will not be concerned or intimidated by the pain. I will shift my attention from the pain to emotional issues. I intend to be in control—not my subconscious mind. I must think psychological at all times, not physical.*
>
> —John E. Sarno, *Healing Back Pain: The Mind-Body Connection*

I would recommend this book to anyone suffering from a physical manifestation of pain or disease. Try to be open to the possibility that your body is sending you a message in an attempt to help you heal. The fact that my physical pain, the distortion in my spine, was possibly a result of repressed emotions, was fascinating to me. It was the first time in my life I even considered that my emotions could affect my body, that there was any connection between my feelings and thoughts and my physical well-being.

I had always taken advantage of my ability to push my body and come to rely on my body as a tool to handle the emotions I felt so deeply all my life.

It became a very exciting time in my life; I felt alive and hopeful. I felt like things were making sense and that there was a deeper meaning and purpose to it all. I became obsessed with the mind-body connection and the healing journey. I couldn't get enough information, and I began to trust the process, and even more importantly, I began to trust the little voice inside that meditation had reconnected me with so beautifully.

An insatiable hunger was born in me, to explore and uncover what needed to be healed. I became less and less afraid of my pain, and more curious about what it was trying to teach me. As Sarno suggested, I intended to be in control, not my subconscious mind.

And so, I went on a quest to find out what was hiding in my subconscious mind. What was I angry about? What was I anxious about? What emotions had I been attempting to ignore? When we become willing to see the truth, the truth reveals itself.

A Memory Rises To The Surface

Early in our relationship, my husband and I took a trip to New York with his parents to see *Jersey Boys* on Broadway. It wasn't until that moment that I felt the impact of my decision to give up acting.

I sat in the audience and choked back the sobs as I watched these beautiful humans on stage doing what I was born to do... perform, dance, sing, act. I mourned the loss of a dream. The lump in my throat throbbed, and tears streamed down my face, as I imagined myself on stage, free and fully expressed... who I was born to be.

I saw the version of me that I had given up. I had convinced myself I didn't want it, didn't need it. He quit acting, and so I quit acting, because I wanted to be with him... Just like in previous relationships, he became my number-one priority, and everything else fell away. I lost myself. I abandoned my dreams. I convinced myself that the desires of my heart were just silly, childish dreams.

After the show, we went out to dinner, and I gorged myself on Bolognese pasta and red wine, pushing down the sadness. I never shared that experience with anyone... I buried it.

Was this what I was angry about? Was I angry that I gave up my dreams? He'd never asked me to... I willingly made the sacrifice. But was I truly at peace with my decision? Was I living the life I was born to live? Could it be possible that my back pain was a result of these repressed emotions?

I continued meditating, I read every book that called to me, and I listened to my inner voice. She grew louder and louder. My back began to heal, as I began to heal. I felt a connection to my soul that I hadn't felt in years. I was overcome with gratitude and an excitement to share everything I was learning.

My Pilates and fitness studio catered to clients interested in high-intensity workouts, but I was feeling called to share my experience of meditation with them. I started ending each class I taught with a gratitude shout-out...

As they sprinted on their mini-trampolines, I would count them down by saying, "On the count of three, I want everyone to shout out what they are grateful for," and the room would burst with enthusiastic declarations of gratitude. My health... my family... exercise... my kids... great food... this studio... and on and on. It lit me up!

I added a mini-meditation during the cool-down portion of each class, introducing them to deep breaths and silence, the same deep breaths and silence that had felt repulsive to me all those years ago. Now, I was the one leading the meditation. Life is funny... Never say never!

I started a women's healing circle and spiritual book study group. I invited guests to come share their stories of holistic health and spirituality. I introduced our high-intensity clients to kundalini yoga. I became a health coach and started coaching clients in our converted storage closet.

My business partner was supportive of my "newfound passions" but also cautioned me to not steer too far away from our "core business." She was comfortable with these additional off-brand offerings as long as I kept our high-intensity offerings the main focus. This was the foundation of our business, after all. But in the same way a child grows out of a pair of shoes as their feet grow, I couldn't stuff myself back into my old shoes.

I tried to appease my business partner, and I kept teaching and promoting all our "core business" classes, but I couldn't stop the runaway train of my spiritual evolution. It no longer felt authentic for me to only focus on the physical aspect of health. It had become glaringly clear that not including the mental, emotional, and spiritual aspects of health and wellness was not an option.

I dreamt of expanding our business. I created an offshoot of the businesses, the yin to the yang. I even had a logo designed for it... We could be one of the first studios to bring together fitness and spirituality. I had a vision that was supported by the little voice inside, encouraging me to follow my heart and say yes to the call of my soul. I saw it as a win-win.

My business partner had a different perspective. Similar to my husband, she was not having a spiritual experience, and did, in fact, accuse me of having a midlife crisis. I didn't totally understand what was happening to me, but I knew it felt right and felt pure.

More Synchronicities

One afternoon, I got a phone call from my hair stylist, Roni. Her salon was in the heart of a beautifully charming main-street-esque area in South Redondo Beach, California. It was this exact street my husband and I had fallen in love with, several years prior; it had sealed the deal for our move from West Hollywood to the South Bay.

Her salon was next to a small corner clothing business, one block up from the beach, with large windows and an ocean view. And she was calling to tell me that that business was closing and there would be a vacancy. She'd thought of me and wondered if I'd be interested in opening a second location.

Only in my most private dreams and visions had I considered another studio. I would daydream about a space near the ocean, with big windows and tons of light, painted with soothing colors, and light wood floors. They say everything that manifests into physical form started out in someone's imagination, and I can say this is true for me.

My business, Allomi, began as a vision in my imagination, a dream, and a heart's desire. As with many dreams, the actual steps necessary to turn the dream into a reality can be daunting and overwhelming. This is why so many dreams stay as dreams. It requires tremendous courage and belief in one's inner knowing to realize them. Some people may think it is a selfish and delusional quest, and that is okay, but that is not my truth.

So, I called the landlord out of curiosity, just to get the details, and as I learned more, my heart started to pound and my body felt a rush of excitement at the possibility. I shared my vision for a holistic healing center, and the landlord seemed very interested.

I got off the phone and ran it by my husband and my parents. The space would require an extensive build-out, and my parents were the contractors for the job. I had their support, so I decided to share the idea with my business partner. She was getting ready to move out of the area, so the plan was for me to be the onsite owner, and she could take care of all the responsibilities that could be handled from a distance.

My vision for this new space was for it to be an extension of our high-intensity business, offering all the complementary services and classes, the yin to the yang. I had a wonderful conversation with my business partner, and although she was not interested in being a part of the sister business, she was supportive as long as I remained invested in our "core business." I left our conversation feeling hopeful and enthusiastic for our next chapter. She gave her blessing for the new business, and it was agreed that I would run that solo.

This opportunity came at the exact same time my soul was calling me to expand my business, and the location was unbelievably perfect! At that point, opening another location had only been a fantasy, not something I was actually ready for. I have taken many leaps on this journey that I haven't felt ready for but that my soul pushed me to take. Everything seemed to be lining up perfectly, and I let the landlord know I was interested in taking over the space.

A couple days later, to my shock and devastation, I opened my email to see a letter from an attorney hired by my business partner, without a warning. *Cease and Desist...*

I was being accused of trying to steal clients for my new business.

This couldn't have been further from the truth. I wanted our business to expand, to offer more! I'd thought she knew that. Our conversation had gone so well, or so I thought. In addition to this crushing accusation, my business partner demanded that we end our business partnership and negotiate a buy-out.

I couldn't believe it. I had been honest and upfront. I had asked for her blessing and shared my vision. Days earlier, she had professed her support, and we'd even hugged in gratitude for the successful business we had created together, celebrating both of our next chapters.

Answering the call of my soul was creating tremendous upheavals in my marriage and business partnership, and I was grief-stricken. But not enough to give up my dream. It felt like my partnership with my soul was taking precedence over all else, and after so many years of ignoring my heart's desires and abandoning the calls of my soul, I wasn't about to give up.

After months of back-and-forth, building attorney fees, disagreeable negotiations, and disheartening conversations, I decided to let go and allow my business partner to buy me out. My husband was furious... He wanted me to keep fighting, to negotiate to buy her out and keep the business.

But I was exhausted and depleted. I couldn't keep fighting. My inner voice told me it was time to let go. I had already signed the lease on the new space, with the understanding it would be an extension of my high-intensity business. And everything changed, just like that.

When we say yes to the call of our soul, oftentimes the Universe has other plans for us. We can resist change and keep fighting to hold on to what is. Or we can surrender to what wants to become.

As painful as it was, there was something in me that feared, if I ignored my soul this time, she might never give me another chance to be who I was born to be. And so, I left my business and the community I had served for the past seven years. It was one of the most painful experiences of my life.

I left without sharing the whole story… I told my community that I had made the choice to embrace my next adventure and new business. I did not tell them about the Cease-and-Desist letter. I did not tell them about the forced buy-out and that I had never intended to leave them. I signed on the dotted line and handed over my keys, never to return. It would be years until I would reconnect with many of the members and have the opportunity to share my story.

In both instances, my marriage and my business, my partners felt abandoned and betrayed. Both partners thought I was being selfish and irresponsible. They were angry that I was revising our agreements and changing the status quo. Looking back, I have compassion for their positions and can understand why they became so resentful. Neither of them was having my experience and didn't understand why I felt so insistent and uncompromising.

I didn't know how to communicate what I was experiencing in a way that would ease the tension. I could only describe it as what felt like a call from my soul that I couldn't say no to. I was willing to risk everything in order to say yes. This was shocking and in vast contradiction to my people-pleasing tendencies, which they had both grown accustomed to.

"You are making the worst business decision anyone could ever make," I heard over and over. I was giving up a perfectly successful business that paid me a monthly salary. A business that he had helped me start... A business we had invested a lot of time and money in and was finally making us money. And my soul wanted me to open a studio where I would teach meditation?

"Nobody cares about meditation. You're not going to be able to make any money. This was not the agreement... You were going to keep your business *and* open this new one."

When it became clear my new business was not going to be a part of my old business, I had to come up with a new name. And after much contemplation, the idea came to me one evening in the shower. Allomi, pronounced *all-o-me*... All Of Me.

This journey I was on was about embracing, accepting, healing and becoming all of me. It was a holistic health and healing studio bringing together movement, meditation, and mindfulness. It was perfect... to me.

It's really hard to convince someone that listening to your soul, your inner knowing, is a reliable way to live. I was speaking a different language, a new language.

It was the beginning of me living a life directed by my inner knowing and soul calling.

The tension grew. The pressure for me to make money at Allomi became greater, and my need to prove that I had made the right decision intensified daily. I would go into the studio, feeling inspired and connected to my purpose and mission, validated by the impact I was having on people's lives. And I would come home and feel deflated and defeated because I wasn't making money.

"Nobody even knows how to pronounce the name of your business. They don't know what it is. At least, in your other business, you had a partner who would reel you back in, when you had a bad idea, and who had a good business mind."

My nightly wine intake increased as I tried to combat the growing dissonance. Had I made a terrible mistake? Should I have fought harder to keep my other business? What if this business fails and I am a failure? What if I'd risked it all to follow a call that turned out to be wrong, after all? I drank more wine.

ೂೀೂೀ

Journal Entry

I am feeling anxiety. I am feeling that kind of fear where my face is hot and I want to escape my feelings. I want to drink. I want to eat. I want to numb. I want to cry. So much doubt creeping in. Did I make a huge mistake?

When we take a leap and say yes to the call of our soul, it triggers the people in our lives, triggers our protector ego... And they try to convince us we're crazy, because they don't see what we see, what our soul self sees.

It's amazing how I can go from feeling so hopeful, so full of life and hope and trust... to feeling filled with anxiety and fear. My face is hot, my head hurts, and I feel a sense of dread. How is it "realistically" possible to go from here to there?

ೂೀೂೀ

Limiting beliefs are reinforced, and the loop continues. I had no tangible evidence I had made the right decision. I had a vision. I had blind faith. I had a fire burning inside that called to me.

But as time went on, no satisfactory evidence to prove my calling was valid and justifiable. Had my "selfish" choice put us in this unpredictable financial position? It ate at me, ate at our marriage.

Journal Entry

I want to numb... but I'm not having wine in the house, so I can't go open a bottle—which is the good news—so, I'm writing. Instead of suppressing and numbing, I am expressing through writing. This is good. This is a good shift.

I feel shut down. I feel angry. I want to stay in faith, but when I look at the numbers, it's so easy to move into self-doubt. I have a chance to shift because I am using healthy tools right now, but the feelings suck. I give my power away, and I sink down into the depths of darkness and doubt.

He's outside now, playing with the kids, and I'm on the couch, writing and wanting to cry. He's the good, fun parent now. I am allowing my anger and dread to take me away from experiencing joy with my kids.

As the painful dissonance grew, my coping strategies to numb the pain grew. I felt like a hypocrite. Here I was, a leader in my community of healing and wellness, and yet I was still struggling with sabotaging behaviors that made me feel deep shame.

I would make deals with myself, try not to drink. The tension in my home became unbearable. But my fear of leaving what I knew felt impossible. Deep in my heart, I knew, if I truly wanted to experience my greatest potential and become the woman I was born to be, I would have to let go of alcohol. It did not serve me. It was a toxic third party, and it did not make me feel like my best self. And I desperately wanted to feel like my best self.

I knew something had to change.

Finally, the pain of self-abandonment through drinking became too great, and I made a decision to let it go.

In December 2019, I was introduced to my friend, teacher, and healer, Christopher Lee Maher, author of *Free For Life: A Navy Seal's Path to Inner Freedom and Outer Peace* and founder of True Body Intelligence. I felt an immediate soul recognition and deep resonance with his teachings.

That Christmas, I went to Florida to spend the holiday with my in-laws. I spent hours by the pool, reading his book, unable to put it down, while downing Prosecco and allowing the tears of resonance to flow down my cheeks. I knew I needed something to help me on this next leg of my journey. And I felt, with all my being, he was the one I was meant to work with. His program required ninety days of abstinence from alcohol, sugar, and caffeine. It was drastic, but I knew I needed something drastic. In February 2020, I committed to his program... My last drink was Superbowl Sunday.

The gap between my husband and me grew. We couldn't figure out how to come together, to find a bridge. It had taken everything I had to finally stop abandoning myself and start healing, and I wasn't willing to turn my back on myself ever again.

The more I discovered the truth of who I was, the more I realized I didn't really enjoy the things I thought I did.

I began feeling quieter and realized I wasn't as much of an extrovert as I had thought. I like alone time. I like quiet. I like not drinking. My diet changed... I no longer enjoyed eating the heavy meals. I became calmer. I didn't want to have people over as much. I slowly became unrecognizable to him.

As the dissonance grew, the tension increased.

And then, Covid happened in March 2020, and the lid on the pot of boiling water exploded.

൙൙൙൙൙

Journal Entry - Sunday, April 5, 2020

I haven't had a drink since February 2. We are in quarantine because of COVID-19. I am still going into the studio every day (except Sunday), to teach live-streaming classes. I have had to take all my business online. First, Instagram Live, and now via Zoom.

"You believe in a Utopia that doesn't exist. You don't live in reality."

When I consider the possibility that there is no utopia, no magic... I am heartbroken. Why, then, do I want it so badly? Why, then, does it feel like I'm living a life that doesn't touch what I'm supposed to be feeling, experiencing? I feel like I'm here to experience magic.

The call for more is so great, it must be answered. I risk it all.

I don't know that I'll be content until I experience the magical utopia my heart believes is possible. Does that mean I'll never be content? Never be truly happy? I've always believed I'm here for more. I've mourned the loss of what I was meant for, only to return to the hope that it's still possible.

I am sober again. Two months... The longest I've been without a drink since I decided to break my twelve years of sobriety, shortly after we started dating, in 2005. I chose that. I knew we wouldn't last, if I stayed sober. There were too many differences, and so, once again, I sacrificed myself.

I didn't know that was what I was doing at the time. I convinced myself that alcohol wasn't the problem, that it was drugs and probably just a phase I was going through... I was only nineteen, for God's sake. That sort of thing happens when you're young. I was fine. I could drink like everyone else.

Alcoholism and addiction ran throughout my family history. I've known for some time now that, in order to have a chance at reaching my full potential, living my wildest dreams, I must release alcohol. So, here I am. Two months sober, with no desire (except for the occasional, "I want to numb and not feel these overwhelming feelings," but even then, I have no desire).

I know it is life and death for me. To numb is to pretend. To pretend is to never know the truth. To never know the truth is living a lie. Living a lie makes me want to drink. And so, I am sober again.

I am forty-five years old, and I want to experience my full potential. I believe in magic. I believe in utopia. Please God, tell me I'm not wrong for believing.

৵৵৵৵

Journal Entry - Tuesday, April 7, 2020

I am reading Untamed *by Glennon Doyle. A book so profound, I wept in the bath and felt like my pain would swallow me, because it resonated so deeply…*

She wrote words I feel like I could have written… They are so true.

I feel like roaring like a lioness to all the men I've given my power to. I have rage inside when I think about all the times I've shrunk, I've given my power away, I've stopped believing in myself, I've pretended, I've kept my mouth shut, I've given them the strings, and I am the puppet. I refuse to give away my strings anymore.

My daughter is so strong—she has not been broken. She holds her strings and refuses to give them to anyone, including me. Will she always hold her strings? If I hold mine and live by example, will she have the strength to hold tightly to hers, never abandoning herself, never sacrificing her truth? I hope so.

I pray that I have the strength to hold them tightly and decide what moves I must make. I am the writer, the director, and the actor. I am the puppet and the puppeteer, the puppet master. I am the master of my show.

"You need someone who will tell you when your ideas are bad. Someone who will tell you the truth"

Really? How does that work? Some people may think it's a brilliant idea. Some may think it's a terrible idea. Who shall I go to? Whom shall I ask?

Aha...! The truth... What is the truth? Only I know my truth. Only I know if my idea is one that I should explore.

There will be mistakes. There will be lessons to learn... But if I wait to have someone else tell me my idea is worthy of exploring, I may never find my gold... It comes from my soul... not theirs, so how will they know? They won't! And here we are again, back to me...

All Of Me... My truth, my idea, my life.

ఴఴఴఴ

Journal Entry - Wednesday, April 8, 2020

I had an aha moment in meditation this morning. "You've lost your mind!"

I realized that losing my mind is completely accurate and *it is a good thing!! I have lost some of the limiting beliefs I have lived with my entire life. I have lost the need to contort myself into what I think others want me to be. I feel free* and *I have lost my mind in the best way possible.*

Ego, the protector but only out of fear.

What does a protector in the energy of love look like? Feel like? Trust. Security. Freedom.

Today my angel card said Gentleness. Don't make any decisions today. You'll know the answer when you return from your gentle retreat.

And so, I trust and stay... Stay with my feelings, stay in this moment, stay in the non-action, and sit with the being.

ఴఴఴఴ

Journal Entry Thursday, April 9, 2020

When I put Dawson to bed, does she notice, when she says, "Night, Daddy," that I say nothing? I don't even whisper good night to her father...

Silently, I am her piggyback ride. I let her say good night while I wait–like a detached chauffeur watching her say goodbye to a stranger. Nothing inside me wants to say good night.

She and I cuddle in bed. I tickle her back. She asks me who I like better, her or her brother, Will. I smile.

"I cannot choose, Dawson. I love you both. You are my favorite girl, and he is my favorite boy."

She asks, "Who is your next favorite? Daddy?"

I stay quiet and return to the point that I love her and her brother more than the whole universe. I am slowly introducing what will be the divorce conversation. "Both your Dad and I love you and your brother more than the whole universe."

You will recognize your worth because I am recognizing mine. I am forty-five years old. I pray it won't take you this long. I don't think it will. You are strong. I will do everything I can to make sure you don't forget how strong you are!

I heard a saying once about being a mother. It's like a little piece of your heart is walking outside of your body for the rest of your life. Protect them, keep them safe, don't let them hurt... Instincts... Motherhood.

When I think about it too much, it suffocates me. I can't breathe; I want to sob. They have so many years of life ahead... So many scary things... I must be brave for them. I must be brave for myself.

My son is going through a hard time right now, being quarantined. He's a social little guy... Loves being at school. He loves playing sports and interacting with his friends and teachers. He is struggling. He feels the tension in the house. He is so sensitive and kind... He has been feeling rage, anger, fear, sadness... He feels it all. He is like me... a sponge absorbing it all.

How can I protect him from feeling it all? Perhaps I will continue to feel it all myself and be brave. Show him we can feel it all and we can be okay. I won't be able to protect him from life... Life happens. Scary things happen. Sad things happen.

I can be steady for him... the calm in the storm, a refuge. I am learning how to be my own refuge. Perhaps that will be my job–to teach him how to be his own refuge.

I breathe. I come back to the present moment. If I go too far outside the present moment, I lose my calm, so I breathe back into the now. I will be okay. I am okay. He will be okay. We will all be okay.

Will he be angry at me, when we tell them we are divorcing? Will he want to live with me? Will he want to live with his dad? Luckily, he is five, so we will decide this for him. I pray we will be able to navigate this without causing more harm to our kids.

I will be steady. I will be consistent. I will keep my ugly, hurtful words to myself. My children will see me handle this with grace and strength. Please God, give me grace and strength.

৵৵৵৵

Up to that point, I was terrified that leaving my marriage would destroy my children. And then, it became glaringly clear that staying in my marriage would destroy my children. My five-year-old, easy-going, happy-go-lucky son was having raging tantrums, and my seven-year-old, bright, beautiful, and wise daughter was pulling chunks of hair out of her head. I was a fool to think the increased tension wasn't greatly affecting my sweet, young children.

And in a moment, a decision that I had tried to avoid making for years was made… I was leaving. If I stayed, this was the example of love and marriage my children would have. And I just couldn't do that to them.

I hadn't been able to make the choice for myself alone. But the love I have for my children gave me the strength to make an impossible decision. I was no longer willing to live a lie. I had to face the truth. I had stayed in that marriage for much longer than I was happy.

Fear can keep you in situations that don't honor you or are not in alignment for a very long time, because the alternative is terrifying, and what's on the other side is unknown. I became willing to walk into the unknown.

ॐॐॐॐ

Chapter 5

The Quest to Understand

There's No Such Thing As "Perfect"

Both my parents had less-than-perfect childhoods. And they grew up in a different time, when parents didn't have the types of conversations that we have with our children today. People just moved on with their lives and made the best of it. They swept things under the rug and pretended like everything was okay, when it most definitely was not.

They didn't ask their children about their feelings or talk about traumatic events. Parents didn't have the self-awareness that we have access to today. So, of course, they didn't ask questions. They were trying to survive. Survival mode, fight or flight, doing the best they could with the tools they had.

My dad was one of four children. When breast cancer took his mom, she left a two-year-old, a six-year-old, a seven-year-old, and a thirteen-year-old without a mother. My dad was the seven-year-old. My grandpa worked two jobs just to make ends meet. No time to grieve the loss of his beloved wife; immediately stepping into the role of a single parent and sole provider to four young children.

My dad's older sister was thirteen and took on the mother-figure role. She was wonderfully nurturing, but growing up without a mom offered unique wounds for each child. And they didn't talk about it. My dad's memories of his mom are minimal. He vaguely remembers her being sick, he vaguely remembers his dad going to the hospital to be with her. And he vaguely remembers his dad coming home without her. And that was that.

My dad grew up feeling loved and supported, with a tremendous amount of respect and appreciation for his dad. But the absence of a mother had to have left particular scars.

My mom's childhood offered its own type of trauma and wounding. Her dad moved their family of four every year for a new, hopeful endeavor, always chasing something. My mom was always the new girl in school, never feeling like she fit in.

Her parents had an awful divorce when she was fourteen, and her father went on to remarry three more times, often prioritizing his new family over her and her younger brother. She never had the relationship with her dad that she craved, always vying for his love and approval, and never fully receiving it. These core wounds caused her self-esteem to suffer from a young age.

That's how generational trauma gets passed down. Her father's own unhealed wounds kept him from being the father she and her brother, Jeff, so desperately wanted and needed. And her mother, like many women, had abandoned herself at the start of their marriage, becoming whom he wanted her to be, and never fully recovering after their divorce. She struggled with her mental well-being, self-medicating with alcohol and pills, and often leaving my mom to feel like she was the parent from a young age.

So, when my parents came together at the ages of sixteen and seventeen, each with their own unique childhood wounds, they fit... They saved each other, and they loved each other in a way both so deeply needed. When they had me in their mid-twenties and my sister seven years later, they vowed to be the "perfect family" and give their children everything they didn't have.

And they did. I had an ideal childhood, with two parents who loved me and who loved each other. They made my sister and me their number-one priority.

I grew up in a nice, middle-class home in Long Beach, California and went to the local private Catholic elementary school. My parents were incredibly supportive and involved. They took me to all my gymnastics practices and meets, dance lessons, and performances. My dad was always the coach of my youth sports teams, and my mom volunteered in the snack shop at school.

When I started acting at the age of ten, my mom drove me to all my auditions and gigs. My entire extended family attended every live performance I had... I always had the largest cheering section.

It baffled me. I had a childhood most people dream about having. My house was the home my friends wanted to gather at, my parents welcoming everyone in with open arms. This is why all my mistakes and failures never made sense to me... never felt justified. How could someone with this childhood end up addicted to crystal methamphetamine and in drug rehab at the young age of nineteen? How could someone whose parents have been married for over fifty years be twice divorced?

Over the years, it caused me a tremendous amount of shame and confusion. It made me feel like there was something even more wrong with me than the people I knew who had obvious reasons for their "bad choices and perceive failures." I didn't have anything tangible to blame my failures on, and therefore, I believed I must be inherently more flawed than most people. This has led me on a quest to understand and get to the bottom of things.

It has taken me years of soul searching and deep dives into my inner child wounds and subconscious beliefs to make sense of it all and to release the shame I carried with me for so long.

When I was three years old, my Uncle Jeff died. He was my mom's younger brother, and he took his own life at the age of twenty-six. I was only three, so my conscious memories of him are limited. But I remember him taking me to a restaurant in Seal Beach, where I sat at the bar on a tall bar stool next to him, and he ordered a Shirley Temple with extra cherries. I remember him giving me my first dog, Coco. I remember he had long, curly hair and a sweet smile. He was an alcoholic and drug addict. I did not know this until later in my life.

And when I was nineteen years old, struggling with a drug addiction of my own, he was the one I talked to, prayed to... He was my guardian angel. I knew he understood the depth of my darkness. I knew he understood the massive shame and loneliness I felt, and it brought me some comfort. I couldn't make sense of how someone like me, who came from the perfect family, could end up a drug addict. I always thought you had to have a messed-up, traumatic childhood to end up addicted to drugs.

The tragic death of my uncle was a traumatic event. But it didn't happen to me. It wasn't trauma that happened to me, not enough to justify my struggles and bad choices, anyway. I don't remember it affecting my life dramatically. My parents didn't make a big deal about it. One day, Uncle Jeff was there, and the next day, he wasn't. And life went on.

It's a delicate conversation to have with a child... Death, that is, especially when it's of this nature. And I think my parents decided there wasn't much to talk about that would make sense to a three-year-old, other than the standard, "Uncle Jeff went to be with God." My mom told me a story later in life about when she told me Uncle Jeff went to be with God. I asked her where God was, and before she could answer me, I said, "Oh, I know. God is in your heart." At three, I knew God was in my heart.

In my search to make sense of my life and my choices, I have asked my parents a lot of questions. Perhaps they could help me gain helpful insight. Were there things that happened in their childhoods that could have affected me? And even further back... Did the experiences of my grandparents and their grandparents affect me?

And were there things in my own childhood that I didn't remember? Were there experiences that could have affected me more deeply than I consciously knew? Were there beliefs that were born and stored in my subconscious that I had no awareness of? And were these beliefs responsible for the paths I had chosen? Paths that made me feel like a failure and a loser? Drug addiction, a trip to rehab, toxic and painful relationships, college dropout, two failed marriages. None of it made sense to me.

I am grateful that my parents have honored this quest of mine, sharing stories with me as an adult that might help me answer some of my life-long questions. My mom shared with me that, at around the time my Uncle Jeff died, my parents experienced an upsetting dip in their marriage; a painful time of disconnect that led to marriage counseling and, ultimately, the resolution to fight for their marriage. Is it possible I felt the energy of their pain and disconnect, despite their loving actions as parents to protect and shelter me from their upset?

I have had a pattern in my life of wanting to save people from their pain, a pattern of choosing codependent relationships. I have chosen people who have experienced trauma and tried to love them into healing, tried to take their pain away with my love.

Is it possible this pattern was born when I was three years old? Did I witness my parents' pain, feel it, and silently offer to help carry the load? Did I take on the responsibility of being the reason my parents were happy? Being the perfect child? Was I the reason they could have the "perfect family" they'd never had? Did I feel the pressure of that role? Was that why I always put so much pressure on myself to be perfect?

This is not about blame. This is about understanding how patterns are born, how trauma gets unknowingly passed down through generations. This is about healing.

At the age of three, our brains register experiences and drive them into the subconscious mind, creating beliefs about the world around us and our role in it.

"The conscious mind is only about five percent of the total mind. It's made up of logic and reasoning as well as our creative abilities, which give rise to our free will. The other ninety-five percent of the total mind is the subconscious mind."

—Dr. Joe Dispenza

sub·con·scious:
Of or concerning the part of the mind of which one is not fully aware but which influences one's actions and feelings.

Whether we have a conscious memory or not, trauma plays out throughout our lives and gets embedded in the nervous system as emotional memory. There may or may not be conscious recollection of situations, but emotional memory has been stored in the nervous system and the body that gets triggered, and we don't even consciously understand why.

Many of us were raised in a culture that promotes the mistrust of our own inner knowing. We are conditioned to place all our faith and trust in external knowing. Parents, teachers, doctors, religious leaders, and politicians… They all know best. Imagine what a different world we would be living in if we were all encouraged, as children, to trust our own inner knowing, and we cultivated this trust into our adulthood!

I want my children to trust themselves; to honor their internal guidance systems. Adults don't always "know what's best." In fact, I think the world would benefit from the wisdom of these preconditioned, unapologetically free beings.

We grow up in a world that teaches us to conform. Be quiet, stay seated, keep your listening ears open. Raise your hand to speak. Sit at a desk for eight hours a day, bombarded with facts that you have to memorize in order to receive a grade, a grade that tells you who you are…

Are you the smart one? If you don't get a good grade, what does that mean? Who are you? Are you worthy? What is the label you are given? And most of the stuff you are being forced to memorize, you could care less about. This is why you daydream… zone out. And you get reprimanded for zoning out, for not paying attention.

My daughter zones out in school a lot. She was also given the "most creative" award at the end of the school year last year. I don't want that to be conditioned out of her. I like that she daydreams and imagines and creates. In fact, daydreaming, imagining, and creating are what brings me much of my joy today, as a grownup! I had to unlearn a lot to give myself permission to return to what came naturally to me so many years ago, as a young girl. This healing journey has been a lot about returning to who I was before the world conditioned her out of me.

I spent my early years conforming, being whom the world wanted me to be. I received praise for performing, being the star, the straight-A student; the precocious, kind, and considerate young girl. I was special and destined for greatness. And I kept it up for as long as I could.

But eventually, the pressure got to me, and I caved. I couldn't uphold my role in our perfect little family anymore. I didn't want to stand out and shine brightly. I didn't want to feel different. I wanted to fit in and be like everyone else.

The rejection wounds from all the times I wasn't chosen as a child actress ate at me and stole the joy I naturally felt from performing, before it became a job and a competition for worthiness. And the decline of my self-esteem from being in a codependent and self-abandoning first major relationship left me raw and vulnerable, desperate to dull my sensitivities and numb my pain.

My role changed, and I became a drug addict and college dropout. I became the crazy older sister... the problem child. My sister earned the role of the easy, emotionally consistent, smart, and successful sibling.

My big feelings and emotions felt like a curse and oftentimes made me feel out of control. My sister never got in trouble growing up. She followed the rules, and not only did she go to college, she went on to earn her master's degree and become a behavioral therapist for kids with special needs.

I was the actress who had stopped acting. I was the sober one who worked as a personal trainer. I was the divorcee. I judged myself harshly for being the "loser" sister. This is a label I gave to myself, but nonetheless a label I carried with me shamefully for many years.

ཀྵཀྵཀྵཀྵ

Journal Entry Tuesday, July 30, 2019

Feel It to Heal It

You have choices. You can distract with something destructive like alcohol, or you can distract with something positive like exercise, or you can just fucking face it and feel it.

This is where I am at: deeply curious about how my lineage has affected me–biologically, mentally, emotionally, spiritually. I can't accept that I am destined to have the same experience previous generations have had with depression and anxiety, either medicated with pharmaceuticals or self-medicated with alcohol and other drugs.

No, I refuse to accept this. I must get to the bottom of it all—the TRUTH. Why is there anxiety and depression? Why is there a long line of "worry warts," always consumed by worst-case scenarios? Why is there addiction and alcoholism? What were they distracting from? What pain were they trying to numb? What is in the lineage that has been passed down, generation to generation that needs to be released?

What is the new story?

ৎ৾ৎ৾ৎ৾ৎ৾

"Empathy with no boundaries is how we become doormats in life."

—Jillian Turecki

Being an empath with no awareness or tools… This is what I have been. But what are healthy boundaries?

How do you know the difference between being loving and supportive and being codependent? When do you stay and accept someone exactly as they are? And when is it damaging to your well-being and you need to leave?

Perhaps when their unhealed wounds, which you, as an empath, have tremendous compassion and empathy for, are causing you pain and causing you to participate in behaviors that lead you to compromise who you truly are.

In a healthy relationship, I imagine we are able to communicate about our core wounds and acknowledge when we feel triggered; we can lovingly hold space and offer security and unconditional love. A place to heal our wounds, not a place that causes more scars.

Is this the difference between a conscious, loving partnership and a toxic, codependent one? A safe place to be triggered, with the opportunity to heal? To be in the energy of empowered ownership and personal responsibility? To be vulnerable and lovingly witnessed? New layers rising to the surface, ready to be healed.

Rejection wounds… Feeling rejected for being me. Needing to adapt, needing to prove myself, to be worthy of love. Why, sweet girl? Why did you not think you deserved better?

I want to be a powerful, embodied woman. I want so desperately to heal, so you can never ever again tell me I am a failure and a loser and have me believe it. Please, God, help me.

⁖⁖⁖⁖

It's taken me a long time to get to where I'm at today. Today, I don't compare myself to my sister. Today, I don't have any role to play, except for my true authentic self. Today, I celebrate the path my life has taken and have a clearer understanding of the choices I have made.

I no longer judge myself harshly, and I have come to truly love myself, all of me. I believe we are all here with a unique Divine mission, and my mission is better served having had all the experiences I've had, especially the ones I thought made me a failure and a loser.

⁖⁖⁖⁖

Writing Prompt

What role did you take on at an early age?
Have you ever felt like you had to compete for worthiness?
How did this affect you?
How does this affect you now?

൙൙൙൙

Uncovering Subconscious Beliefs

Somewhere along the way, I formed a belief that I had to choose between scenarios. I thought I had to choose between being who I was born to be or being in love. Between being all of me or being in a relationship.

This was not a conscious belief, but it is evidenced by many of my choices. When I met my first husband, at the age of twenty-one, I was two years sober and working as a secretary. When we met, my world revolved around my recovery and the people I knew in the 12-Step rooms. And although there were many beautiful gifts from that time in my life, I was certainly not embodying all of me.

When I made the choice to start dancing and acting again, more of me started to come back to life, and I felt like I had to leave that marriage. My first husband was very supportive. He never once asked me to give up acting or pursuing my dreams. But there was something inside, this invisible choice I thought I had to make. Be all of me... or stay married to him.

I remember sobbing on the floor of my living room, praying to God, "Please, God, help me not want more". I wanted to be satisfied with my life…I wanted to silence the inner callings for more… but they couldn't be silenced.

And so, I chose scenario two and got divorced. And for a time, I felt liberated and hopeful. I was pursuing my dreams of performing again, and I felt alive. But eventually, it wasn't enough, and I started to feel lonely, like something was missing…

I always have. What I have come to understand is that what was missing was a deep connection to myself and a self-love that needed to be cultivated. No amount of performing and no romantic relationship would satisfy the feeling I was searching for, which could only be found by truly knowing and loving myself. Today, I believe the hopeful romantic in me, who longs for love and partnership, and the free-spirited wild-woman, who loves her independence and creative expression, can happily coexist, as long as I am embodying all of who I was born to be and am being true to myself.

For most of my life, it has felt like I have two opposing voices living inside my head. One voice is loving and encouraging, and the other is nasty and critical. There are times when I feel confident and carefree. And other times when I feel fearful and incredibly insecure.

In my one-woman show, *Waking Up to All Of Me*, I brought this internal opposition to life through the two main characters, Ego and Soul. I have come to understand this opposition as the contrast in my alignment.

Who is running the show? Ego or Soul? Ego has a job, and it is to protect me from harm and keep me safe at all times. He uses tactics that are fear-based and controlling. Soul also has a job, which is to help me live the life I was born to live. She is all-knowing and unconditionally loving.

She is my higher self, my true soul self, strong and graceful, wise and kind. She is embodied.

When she is running the show, I feel calm and reassured, peaceful and confident that I am right where I am supposed to be. I know I am lovingly supported and guided all the time. When Ego is running the show, I experience self-doubt and feel anxious and fearful. My body feels contracted, and my chest feels tight.

I like it when Soul is driving the car. I thank Ego for his good intentions, but I remind him that he is no longer invited to drive the car, that he may sit in the back seat, with his hands far away from the steering wheel. I tell him we tried it his way, and now, I'm ready to try it her way!

Daydreaming with Ego and Soul

When I am in alignment with my soul, I enjoy daydreaming about living in a beautiful house in Southern California, overlooking the ocean, with a large, grassy lawn where my son can play lacrosse, and my daughter can dance. It has a pool and spa where we can all laugh and play together, on Sunday Family Fundays… with music playing, my man grilling burgers, and maybe even a dog… Yeah, a dog! They bring so much love.

And since I have plenty of money and will be home a lot, writing my books and leading my virtual and in-person women's retreats in the detached two-story studio in the backyard, the dog can be there with me, licking my legs while I write. Looking out at the ocean, warm breeze blowing through the open windows, feeling so grateful and peaceful.

I breathe a deep sigh of satisfaction... I did it... My dreams came true... It was all worth it... We got through some really hard things, but here we are.

Oh, I like it when I am in alignment with my soul. Because, when ego is driving the car, I'm out of money and back living with my parents. Or worse, living in the back house of my ex-husband's and his girlfriend's bigger, nicer house, working at a Curves down the street, because I'm too old and my body hurts too much to teach cardio dance classes anymore. I don't have a college degree, so the only thing I can do is teach old ladies' gentle calisthenics. And I'll still be single, an old maid, and my kids will live in the front, bigger, nicer house with their dad and his girlfriend. They'll come visit me in the back house, pitying me for the failure I've become. And my ex-husband will be nice, only sometimes poking me about how he told me so. And he doesn't need to say anymore, because here I am, living in his back house, teaching at Curves.

Oh, I like it so much better when I am in alignment with my soul, and she is driving the car. I feel like a different woman, like the woman I was born to be. I feel confident... like a fucking rockstar...

Not like the fucking rockstar I felt like at age nineteen, when I tried crystal meth for the first time... But like a real rockstar, like the kind where I walk confidently down the street, and people look up and notice me, because they feel the magnetic energy I am embodying. When ego is in charge, I walk down the street and the people don't even lift their heads to notice me. They don't feel the magnetizing pull to look up... They just keep drinking their coffee and gossiping with their friends.

These are the tricks my mind plays on me. And I'm pretty sure I'm not alone. And this is why I make it a priority on a daily basis to practice all the tools that keep me in alignment with my true soul self.

I notice when Mr. Ego tries to butt in, and I kindly remind him of his place.

∽∽∽∽

Journal Entry: Creating My One-Woman Show

What if my deepest heart's desire to be on stage and tell my story is more valuable than I thought? What if it inspires others to have the courage to do the same. Why do people like to be entertained? They feel inspired. They feel moved. You hear that all the time... "I felt moved!"

What does that mean? Moved how? Moved where? Perhaps, they get to experience something they won't allow themselves to create in their own lives, through a character on stage or on the screen. They feel the energy of inspiration. They get to move their energy, their emotions, by simply witnessing someone else do it. A vehicle for movement... a vehicle for expression... a vehicle for healing.

Wow, what if my deepest, truest heart's desires help initiate healing? What if they are as valuable as someone who went to school for a really long time and studied really hard and earned degrees? What if my little college-dropout self was just as valuable as those "educated" people... those "smart" and "important" people? What if my gifts were just as important?

What if I didn't have to keep putting my deepest heart's desires in a box, packed up in the dark, lonely attic–just memories of what could have been? What if I didn't have to deny it and try to find a more "reasonable and legitimate" career?

I can hear the old stories, the comparisons that made me feel "less than." My sister earned her master's degree and helps kids with autism. I was an actress who dropped out of college. It always sounded so superficial. What was I contributing to the world by acting?

It's so interesting... Where did I get that belief? Maybe the world around me? An actress? She and the rest of Los Angeles... Hahaha... What else is she?

I didn't understand the value of my gifts then, and just like everyone else in the world, I wanted to matter... I wanted to make a difference. When I became an entrepreneur and business owner, it gave me an identity that felt more valuable, worthy, credible. In my mind, it made up for my lack of education.

But the little voice that longed to express herself as a performer and entertainer never fully went away. I could tap into it as a fitness instructor, but it never fully satisfied the innate desire I was born with. And I dreamed of being on stage once again.

I created a one-woman show about the battle between Ego and Soul, and I entertained people and educated them. I felt the value of my gifts, and it felt really good.

☙☙☙☙

Chapter 6
Strong Enough to Embrace the Truth

The first time I looked into my daughter's eyes, it felt like something was born in me that I hadn't known existed. I had never been the kind of woman who was crazy about other people's children–never babysat, never wanted to babysit–so I wasn't sure what motherhood would feel like. I knew I wanted to be a mother, but I had no frame of reference for this kind of love.

My daughter, Dawson, arrived two weeks early. My first contraction came in the middle of the night, and according to all the birth classes my husband and I had taken, I was to start timing my contractions and go to the hospital when they were a certain number of minutes apart.

Before I could even start timing them, they were coming in waves, one right after the other, one barely crashing into the shore before another one rolled in. They tell you to come up with a birth plan, but to have some flexibility, because you aren't in total control of how things go. I hadn't planned on having a natural birth… In fact, my birth plan included an epidural as soon as they could give me one.

I remember squeezing my mom's hand on one side of me and looking up at my husband on the other side, pleading with him to tell me when the anesthesiologist was coming with the relief. He and the nurses kept assuring me he was on his way. Apparently, they were quite busy that morning... Lots of little souls decided to join us that day... He was assisting the other mamas-to-be.

I dilated all the way to ten... I rode those waves one right after the other, knowing on the other side would be my beautiful baby girl. It would all be worth it!

The anesthesiologist finally did come after I had already dilated all the way and offered to give me the epidural. I didn't really need it, but I gladly accepted it, enjoying the short respite before the hard job of pushing began.

They had to take my daughter to the nursery–she needed some help breathing because of her early arrival. My panic was eased by my sheer exhaustion and also believing they would have taken her to the NICU, if it had been more serious. They tried to ease my worries and encouraged me to enjoy the breakfast they were serving. I remember it vividly: the fluffy pancakes with warm syrup tasted so good after what felt like running a marathon.

She had to stay in the nursery that first night, while I stayed in the hospital room. She was a little jaundiced, and they wanted to monitor her under the lights overnight. I had also been jaundiced at birth, so this didn't alarm me too much. The nurses told me I could sleep, that they would feed her and get up with her throughout the night. But something had been born in me... a strength and fierceness I had never known... the Great Mother in me.

My husband snored peacefully on the pull-out couch bed in my hospital room as I pumped what little milk I had into tiny little bottles. I remember, in the middle of the night, walking down the hospital corridor to the nursery where my girl, Dawson, was, clasping the back of my gown, swelling with the pride and purpose of being a mother... *Dawson's mother*.

The words "I am a mom" repeated loudly in my head, over and over. This incredible soul had chosen me. And I wasn't about to sleep on the job her very first night here. I would be there by her side. I would be the one to soothe her when she cried and feed her when she was hungry. She needed me, and I needed her.

Although I wouldn't have my spiritual awakening for two more years, after her brother, Will, was born, I do believe her birth was the beginning of me waking up to all of me. I imagine her sweet soul, watching me from another realm, waiting for the perfect time to join me here on Earth, choosing that exact moment because she knew how much I needed her... needed her to remind me of who I was.

The strength that was born in me the day she became my daughter is the same strength that has allowed me to embrace the truth of who I am and why I am here. It has not been an easy road, and there have been many days I have felt weak and discouraged, days when it has felt too big, too much to handle... And then, I am reminded of my strength, and I find my resilience.

That same sense of pride and purpose I felt, walking down the hospital corridor some eleven years ago, rises up inside of me with a ferocity, and once again, I feel unstoppable. I am her, and she is me. And I will model for her a woman who knows who she is. A woman who is embodying all of who she was born to be. And this is what she will know for herself, because of my strength, the strength she gave to me. This beautiful cycle. A new cycle begins.

Part of the journey of remembering starts with realizing how very far away you've gotten from your true self and how much you have forgotten who you really are. This is a painful realization, and one that I tried to ignore for many years. One of the tools I used to try to ignore the truth was drinking alcohol. I wasn't ready to accept my assignment; I wanted to blend in and be like everyone else. I had a lot of fun. And I had many moments of shame, of not being who I knew I was born to be.

In 2011, I opened my first business, HIP Studio, the high-intensity Pilates and fitness studio I co-owned in Hermosa Beach, California. Opening weekend was filled with celebration and pride, and also with shame and sadness.

My business partner and I went out with our men to celebrate our first day of being in business! It started innocently enough, having some afternoon cocktails in the sun, and the more fun we had, the more we wanted to have. It became a pub crawl of sorts, ending at an Italian restaurant for dinner with red wine.

I hadn't eaten all day, drinking hard alcohol in the sun, and on the drive home from the restaurant that night, I got sick... Pull over your car, and throw up out the window sick.

The next morning, I was scheduled to teach a couple classes for our new members, and I couldn't. The nausea carried into the morning, along with the pounding headache, and we got another teacher to step in. I hated myself for not being able to show up that morning.

Now, that wasn't the norm for me, and the next seven years, while I was the co-owner of that studio, were filled with me showing up as my best self, a responsible and proud owner. But I will tell you, that experience of not being able to show up on opening weekend because of the way I had used alcohol stuck with me, and I carried the shame with me.

I tried to convince myself that it wasn't a big deal… I hadn't eaten, I hadn't gotten a lot of sleep the night before, everyone drank that much, and we were celebrating, blah blah blah. But deep inside, I knew the truth. I knew that drinking alcohol was robbing me of the ability to truly step into who I was born to be.

But it would take me some time to become willing to let it go and fully say yes. I was afraid to let go of all the things that would go with it, if I said goodbye to alcohol. I couldn't see, at the time, all the things I would be opening myself to receive in its place. More authentic, more aligned experiences and relationships.

Authenticity is medicine. Resonance is medicine. Hearing our truth is medicine. Living our truth is medicine.

∽∽∽∽

Journal Entry - Sunday, April 28, 2019

I joined a women's group coaching course, and we had our first call yesterday. I said yes because I want to continue to evolve and truly step into my greatness. I said yes without really knowing what I was getting into. I need to be in the company of other high-vibrating souls saying yes to their call.

Energy is a crazy thing. Just yesterday, I felt stuck and uninspired, restless. And this morning, I am excited about the adventure I'm on right now, about the possibility of creating something from the depths of my heart's desires. It makes me want to weep for some reason.

Yesterday, when I shared my vision, "I want to use all-of-me to inspire, empower, educate, and entertain," I was encouraged to dive deeper into it, to get curious and explore the possibilities. It felt like permission to listen to my deepest heart's desires.

Nobody said, "That's not very realistic… You should just focus on coaching and making money coaching." Nobody said, "You really need to focus on what is practical and stop dreaming." Nobody said that. In fact, I was encouraged to paint a picture of what is possible and asked to explore writing a play and songs…

I feel like weeping, just thinking about the possibilities.

I realized this morning I get stuck and feel hopeless when I think that achieving my greatest desires is dependent on someone else… On someone outside of myself seeing my truth and giving me a lucky break.

Old patterns, giving my power away… Thinking something outside of me is responsible for my success. That is when I feel helpless. I remind myself that I am a powerful creator… And when I align energetically and spiritually, I create possibilities and call in the right people.

My spiritual awakening in 2014 opened me up to a whole new world of what was possible. It reconnected me to the part of me that knows anything is possible and that my dreams and desires are clues to my destiny.

The more I moved closer to my true soul self, the things that were not a match to that started to feel more uncomfortable.

ೞೞೞೞ

Journal Entry - April 12, 2018

I haven't had a drink since last Sunday (today is Friday). I am grateful. I have prayed for a shift, for the willingness to release, to step off the wheel, to break the cycle of addiction.

I drink wine every night — not this week. I have a deep heart's desire to stop this cycle and create a new normal, a new habit, a miracle of transformation. I feel good. I feel clear. I feel grateful. I am receiving messages of confirmation.

Yesterday, when I was picking up my vitamins and supplements, I heard a woman talking about rashes... about emotions coming out through the skin in a rash.

Okay, I'm listening. My rash has been with me since February. It is April 12, and it has not gone away. Clearly, my body is talking to me.

I've been here before with my back. Thank you, body, for helping me to heal.

ೞೞೞೞ

Journal Entry - Sunday, June 30, 2019

Love can heal anything... I've always felt that. And I still do believe that. But it's not my love for someone; it has to be their love for themselves.

I must teach my children that... I must love myself and lead by example. I do love myself... I am kind and passionate, sensitive and hopeful, emotional and deep-feeling, relatable and compassionate. I have a kind heart and a bright light.

I have numbed my deep feelings over the years. I have been disappointed by other people's lack of love, lack of hope. I have been hurt by other people's actions that have nothing to do with me.

We choose people who reflect our limiting beliefs and trigger our core wounds. Perhaps, it is an unconscious attempt to heal these wounds. But when we choose from our wounded place, it becomes a vicious cycle, until we can see the truth and choose to heal ourselves.

ട്ട‌ട്ട‌ട്ട‌ട്ട

In June 2020, I made the most difficult decision of my life thus far. I left my marriage. I said yes to me. My kids were five and seven. I had come to believe that I deserved better, that we all deserved better. I deserve to be loved in a way that feels aligned with the woman I was born to be, the woman I am. I want this for me, and I want this for my children.

Relationships are an opportunity to look in the mirror… a place where our beliefs are reflected back to us through our partner, beliefs we have about ourselves. Core wounds play out in a dance between two people. Where there is no awareness, there is blame, there is pain.

I am single now. I am allowing myself time to heal, to recognize and release old beliefs, and to form new, healthier beliefs based in self-love and worthiness. I am creating a life that reflects my most amazing qualities.

The fragmented pieces are coming back into wholeness. That sweet little girl who had her heart broken, taking it all so very personally, making it her identity: I am her. And I am the embodied woman who said yes to the call of her soul and bravely stepped into the unknown, fiercely believing in herself and in her worthiness.

I am the little girl who dazzled the important grown-ups at the age of ten, and also the teenager who felt betrayed and crushed in her first relationship at the age of sixteen. I am the girl who danced and sang her heart out, full of fire and spice. I am the girl who knew she was special, and I am also the girl who didn't believe she was special enough and stayed in relationships where she was betrayed and treated poorly.

The truth is I am stronger than I often give myself credit for. I am the woman who has been courageous enough to believe that her dreams are possible, who has taken bold steps in the direction of her dreams, in spite of all the fear and doubt... And that is something to be proud of.

The Divorce

Journal Entry - June 2, 2020

My daughter, Dawson, is seven and my son, Will, is five. It's Tuesday night at 10 p.m. We are arguing again!

I can't pull myself away. I know better! My kids are still up, and it's a school night. They are playing in our bathroom, taking videos of each other with my phone. I have given my five- and seven-year-old my phone, so I can continue this futile attempt to bridge the gap, a gap that is widening by the day. I am desperate. Deep sadness pushing up against rage. A lifetime of feeling misunderstood. A lifetime of feeling different. I am terrified. I can't see how this is going to get better.

I'm watching myself, and there is a deep part of me who knows I should walk away, go tuck the kids into bed. I'm lying to myself... telling myself they can't hear.

They can hear us... They know... They are much smarter than I allow myself to believe.

ぬぬぬぬ

Journal Entry - June 9, 2020

"It's time to end this and get a divorce."

The impossible frustration had exploded, and neither of us felt any hope in that moment.

We had been talking about it for years. The dissonance in our marriage was obvious and growing by the day. Tension in the house was suffocating. It was time. As terrified as I was, I knew I had no choice.

The guilt I felt for potentially ruining my children's lives was so heavy, but I knew that staying, keeping them in this house, was even more damaging than leaving.

I took Dawson to the car wash. She asked me for a coin to put into the fountain. She made a wish that her dad and I wouldn't fight anymore.

Will says he doesn't like it when we fight. That we close our door, but he can still hear us, and he turns the TV up, so he can't hear us. He's five years old...

How have I allowed this to happen? How am I here? How did I get here? How did I let myself get here?

ぬぬぬぬ

Painful relationships can be the greatest catalyst to our remembering, or they can be the demise of our greatest destiny.

It is our choice. It takes a tremendous amount of courage to listen to the voice that is trying to pull you out of the depths of demise and throw you onto the road to remembering.

Journal Entry - June 10, 2020

I took the kids and stayed at my parents for the night

Journal Entry - June 20, 2020

I taught Plyojam today online. I keep showing up.

I have shown up for my community this whole time, but what I didn't realize was that my need to show up for them saved me through one of the darkest times in my life.

Having to show up for my kids and for the Allomi community gave me the strength I needed to keep going. It gave me purpose.

Journal Entry - June 21, 2020

We officially moved into my parents' house. They turned my mom's office into Will's bedroom... But Dawson doesn't really ever sleep in her room... They sleep together in this big bed in Will's new room.

Journal Entry - June 22, 2020

I took the kids to the park across the street from my parents'. I take them to the park a lot.

ଈଈଈଈ

Journal Entry - June 24, 2020

My car got smashed in front of Allomi by a car that accidentally reversed around the corner.
Really, God? Sometimes, life doesn't make sense.

ଈଈଈଈ

Journal Entry - June 30, 2020

I went over to our house today, his house, to play with the kids. We put on a good face for the kids.
I am grateful and relieved to not be fighting. I feel like I can breathe.

ଈଈଈଈ

Journal Entry - July 4, 2020

We went to a neighbor friend's house to celebrate the Fourth of July. I can't believe I was able to be there, alcohol free for only five months—at this party, newly separated, newly moved out... for my kids. I wanted it to be as seamless as possible. I have so much guilt for the pain I have caused them, and will continue to cause them, as I walk forward toward the end of our family unit as we know it.

ଈଈଈଈ

Journal Entry - July 9, 2020

The therapist suggested we separate for three weeks. Today is three weeks, and I don't see a way for us to make it work. I told him it's officially over.

The kids are with him today. I stopped by this morning to wake up the kids before I taught my class.

This is one of the hardest parts of the separation. I wake my kids up every single morning and tuck them into bed every single night. I can't imagine a life where I don't get to do that.

⚜⚜⚜⚜

Journal Entry - July 10, 2020

I'm taking one step at a time. The voice of self-doubt creeps in. I've taken the leap. I want tangible proof I am making the right choice.

Breathing. Quiet time in the car... Longer commute in the car; time to listen to podcasts. I want to fast-forward through these icky painful parts and get to the good stuff.

But what if I just said, "Yes, bring it on. Let me just dive into these icky parts..." Slow motion instead of fast forward. I don't want to bypass anything... I don't want to get out of this relationship to just jump into another self-abandoning relationship.

Some fond, cherished moments in these painful transitions... I know there is another side. I won't feel like this forever. Everything I go through is so I can teach about it. I want to be the living example of a woman on a spiritual journey, listening to her heart, going through some tough stuff, being okay, and growing through it.

Journal Entry - August 10, 2020

I took the kids to lunch, and Will got upset about something and said, "I can't wait until I don't have to be with you."

Knife in my heart... Tough stuff a five-year-old is going through.

I try not to take it personally. I know he loves me. Please God, give me strength.

I hold back my tears and try to be strong for him. "I know, sweetheart, you're feeling frustrated and angry. I'm sorry. I love you."

Today, I sent in my divorce papers. There will be more tough moments like this. I can do this. I must be strong for my kids, for myself.

Journal Entry - August 11, 2020

Today was a good day. We're at my parents' house, and the kids were laughing and playing on the cardboard box "bed" they made. They seem to be doing okay.

I am so grateful for my parents. It is such a blessing to be in this home, with their love and support for me and the kids.

It is a sad time and a happy time. It's summer, and it's hot, and everything is shut down because of Covid... Thank God for my parents' pool!

Journal Entry - August 30, 2020

My kids went back East with their Dad… Their first vacation without me… The first time they flew across the country without me.

I pray for their safety, and I surrender. Otherwise, the fear and sadness will consume me; it will be too much.

They celebrated Will's sixth birthday on this trip. For as painful as it got between us, I will forever be grateful that we have always included each other by sending pictures and videos of the kids, when we are apart.

He sent me videos… The East Coast crew singing happy birthday to Will. I'm grateful for the videos, and it's really hard to not be there with him, singing to him, celebrating with him.

ಈಈಈಈ

Journal Entry - September 8, 2020

First day of school… Covid is still here… Will is in kindergarten and Dawson is in second grade. Will gets to go to "day-care distance learning" on campus, but Dawson is in a pod at a classmate's house. I am so grateful they get to go to school.

I am living with my parents, until I can afford a place of my own and sort out the details of the divorce. We are splitting time with the kids, and I am trying to adjust to the nights they are with their dad. There are many nights I cry myself to sleep, missing them, grieving what was.

My parents are so wonderful to allow us into their home, but it's a lot, and the extra energy in the house is evident. My kids are five and seven, and their parents are going through a divorce… So, in addition to just being kids, they are dealing with their own feelings about this transition to our new normal.

I am doing my best, doing what I think is the right thing to support them. They are loud; they bring chaos into the home. Tons of energy, noise, play.

I feel like I am more anxious with the kids, worried about how their extra energy is affecting the home that has been accustomed to only two older adults and two dogs.

I vacillate between being so grateful to be here, with some sense of normalcy for my kids, a family, a support system… And my desire to have my own space, where I am the one responsible for the energy in the house, and I'm not worried about how my kids are affecting anyone but me.

ঔঔঔঔ

Journal Entry: The Inner Knowing 2021

It has taken me forty-six years to get to this place of absolute trust in my own inner knowing. It has taken me a lifetime of believing that other people know better, of relying on other people's acceptance, agreement, and validation to determine what is true for me.

I have lived to please others, to be accepted by others, to be validated by others. In the process, I lost myself.

ঔঔঔঔ

Learning to Trust the Inner Voice Again

It's a really interesting process, when you start to trust the inner voice inside, and everyone in your life is used to you relying on their approval, their guidance, and their validation. All of a sudden, this dark night of the soul, this spiritual awakening, has you listening to your own inner knowing above anything else.

It's quite shocking, really, to the people in your life. It's very destabilizing and commonly causes much dissonance in relationships.

Uncertainty and Faith

They say the transformational journey is not for the faint of heart. I will add that, unless you feel the call of your soul magnetically pulling into this journey, and unless you feel you absolutely must travel this path, don't do it. Stay home on your couch, drinking your wine and watching Netflix.

But if you must travel this path and your soul calls to you, begging you to dive deep into the truth of who you are and why you are here, then I am here to hold your hand and tell you it's all going to be okay, and it's all worth it, that you are worth it.

There are going to be times of tremendous uncertainty and fear; times when all you have is your faith and vision for a greater reality. There is this in-between part after you've jumped off the cliff, when nothing seems to make sense, and you doubt every decision you've made.

I had this experience while I was living with my parents after my divorce. I had taken the leap, left my marriage, and trusted that what I truly desired was out there, waiting for me. Yet I had nothing to show for it. I felt lost again.

Had this all been a huge mistake, I wondered. Would I have been better off staying at my old business, staying in my marriage, just staying? Was I just the kind of person who always thought the grass was greener? Did I believe in a utopia that doesn't exist? Was I selfish? Was I living in la-la land? Was I wrong?

The agony of doubt is so heavy, so all consuming.

∽∽∽∽

Journal Entry - Thursday, September 24, 2020

I've been out of the house since the end of June, living with my parents. We are getting a divorce. It's happening—it's finally happening.

God, how many times I've cried, wishing and praying for freedom and happiness, knowing in my heart it wasn't possible with him, but too terrified to leave. I was so afraid, so angry, so sad, so hopeless. We speak different languages. I feel there is so much to repair. One of the many things we don't agree on, and so, I must go. My heart has much love to give... It has been wounded, and it needs time to heal.

The kids are doing well, as well as they can be doing in the middle of their parents' divorce and a global pandemic. Their dad and I have been able to get along so far. We are amicable in our communication and in front of the kids. Thank you, God. I didn't expect this, and I am grateful. Sometimes, I even forget how bad I felt, because I've had peace for some time now.

"Aren't you lonely?" he asked, convinced I am already dating someone. I am not.

"I've been lonely for years. I'm happy because I'm at peace. No more fighting, no more tension."

My parents have been amazing... such an incredible support for me and the kiddos. Will and Papa have such a special bond. I love watching them snuggle together, watching the Dodgers game. My kids and I feel at home and safe. I am grateful.

ของของของของ

Journal Entry - October 15, 2020

I woke up this morning feeling grateful, feeling the joy in my body from all the beautiful moments of the weekend. There is a song by Shawn Mendes, "Never Be Alone." My daughter and I love to listen to Shawn Mendes in the car.

Yesterday, she told me that, when she was back east with her dad this summer, she never felt alone, because I am always in her heart. This girl... A love fest with her... I feel so in love.

I woke up feeling rested and awake... a feeling of hopeful anticipation for what the day will bring. The air feels cool and crisp... It feels good... It feels like something new... A birth of something new.

The drive to school this morning, so full of love and celebration... Blasting the music, singing the songs together, dancing in our seats... I can see their smiling faces in my rearview mirror, and I feel overwhelmed with appreciation for what is.

They hug my parents goodbye before we leave. So much love is exchanged. I have felt eager to move, to have my own space, I know it will happen... Today, I relish the gifts my kids and I are receiving from my parents, from this time.

The painful memory of their parents' divorce is also filled with happy moments, moments of love and connection. It makes me trust even more, the mysterious ways God works. Today is a good day, filled with many things that bring me joy.

∽∽∽∽

Part of being a human being is experiencing the fluctuation of feelings and emotions. Some people have more consistent emotions, and some people have more ups and downs. Growing up, my sister had more consistent emotions, or at least that's what I perceived. I compared myself to her and felt less-than for my messy emotions.

As a highly sensitive being, I have tended to experience highs and lows in a way that has made me feel more flawed or fragile than other people. I wear my emotions on my face, and this has made me feel less-than for some reason. I think it's because I didn't understand myself like I do today. I didn't feel like I had control over the way life circumstances affected me. I felt at life's mercy, and this is not an empowering place to live.

Today, I recognize my tendency to experience fluctuating emotions, not as a flaw, but as a part of my unique experience of life. The more I am able to be the observer and witness my emotions and responses to circumstances, without attaching to them, the better I feel.

One day, I can be feeling peaceful and grateful, like all is well with the world, and the very next day, I can dip into fear and worry, focused on all the things that aren't the ways I want them to be. I ride the waves and come back to the present moment, using all my tools.

Riding the Waves

Oftentimes, after we take a big leap into the unknown, self-doubt creeps in. The in-between phase, learning to trust our inner knowing as we await tangible evidence that will, once and for all, convince us we made the right decision. We can experience impatience and extreme discomfort.

This is when we double down on all the things that increase our faith and bring us into alignment with our true soul self. I meditate, pray, dance, write, breathe, listen to uplifting and affirming podcasts, work with a mentor, serve others, and connect with other like-minded souls who are on this path of becoming who they were born to be.

❦❦❦❦

Journal Entry - Monday, November 16, 2020

I am at the studio, and I am feeling very angry, sad, depressed, and tired. I am experiencing such discomfort, romanticizing the past, wanting to escape my feelings today.

I'm living with my parents. They were drinking wine last night... I was wishing I could drink with them... The red wine looked so good... Oh, how I wanted to sit on the couch and disappear into a bottle of wine. The problem is... I would wake up the next morning and feel like shit, hate myself, and be even worse off than I am now. Now, I am sober, and because of that, I have choice. I can sit in the uncomfortable feelings. I know they will pass. They always do.

Divorce is tough and tricky. Just when you think you're completely at peace with it, the kids go on a trip with their dad, but you don't go, and you find yourself sobbing, thinking about all the family vacations you won't take together and the trips they'll take with him and another woman, who is playing the role of "Mom."

It is painful... seeing another woman in that role... seeing your children relate to another woman in that way, in a home that once was yours. Seeing your children in "family" pictures that don't include you.

These are the things you can't prepare yourself for. These are the moments you have to breathe and cry and allow the pain to move through and wash over you. You have to remind yourself of all the reasons divorce was the only answer.

I still haven't met someone. It's moments like these when I wonder if I ever will, and the self-pity feels gross, but it's how I feel in this moment. Everything has purpose; everything happens in Divine timing. How can I believe this for some of my life but not all of my life?

ॐॐॐॐ

It's All About Alignment

I know what my gifts are, and I don't have unlimited time and energy, so I want to use the time and energy I do have by using my gifts in their greatest capacity.

We humans are quite funny... We entertain ourselves with all kinds of speculations. Our brains feel like they are on the spin cycle of a washing machine, and we exhaust ourselves, playing out all the scenarios. And quite honestly, once I surrender to the unknown, I can relax in the waiting period. It's the worry that causes irritation and suffering. But when I can sit in the knowing that it's coming and will be beautiful and worth it, I can actually just chill the fuck out and enjoy the moment.

When I left my first business, I felt like I needed to prove my worth by doing both my job and my business partner's job. I wanted to prove I was smart enough to run a business by myself and do it all. A big reason I felt this way was because my gifts alone did not seem to merit as much value as what she contributed. This was reinforced by her resentment and accusation that she was doing more.

I was equally invested in serving our community and supporting our members on their health and wellness journey, but the way I did that was different from the way she did that. So, I wanted to prove to myself, to her, and to my husband that I was capable, that I could do it all by myself and had what it took to run a business. I wanted to prove that me being half owner mattered and helped the business be successful, it wasn't just her "business mind" that made us successful. There are other, less tangible contributions that are equally important.

I opened Allomi in January 2018, after selling my half of the business. I was consumed with a passion and a calling to create a healing sanctuary that brings together everything I had learned, everything that was helping me to heal... movement, meditation and mindfulness; physical, emotional, mental, and spiritual wellness. I felt a blend of passion and purpose, as well as pressure to prove myself.

Allomi became a very special and impactful little studio. I called in so many beautiful healers and teachers to share their gifts, as well as a community to serve. I manifested the vision and became a version of myself who felt really proud of what she had created.

After five years of being a solo entrepreneur, navigating a global pandemic and a divorce, I felt the call to expand even more. I no longer needed to prove my worth to anyone, and, quite frankly, I was tired of carrying the weight of running a brick-and-mortar on my own. I started dreaming of new possibilities and spent a lot of time praying and meditating on how the next chapter would unfold.

I considered bringing in a partner, I rented space out to other businesses, I contemplated closing altogether, and I thought of hiring support to handle the tasks that were not the greatest use of my gifts. I asked God for a sign and some clear direction. And then, I received an email from my landlord asking me to sign another long-term lease, as I had been going month-to-month after my initial lease term ended.

Her email was the sign I was asking for… It was time to make a decision. I started having conversations with some close friends about my difficult choice. When I thought about signing another long-term lease, I felt anxious and restricted. When I thought about leaving my business, I felt simultaneous sadness and freedom.

After a conversation with a close friend about my options, she confided in me that she had been praying for a sign about a new business she was wanting to manifest. She and her partner wanted to open a healing center and had been looking at locations.

Wow! Could this be my answer? Was I meant to hand over my lease to my friend and her new healing center? Was I ready to let go and step into the next level of expansion I was feeling called into?

One of the things that felt sad to me was leaving the community I had come to serve, but this new possibility would still allow the community to have a place to heal and grow. They say God works in mysterious ways, and this potential transition was definitely evidence of that.

Whenever I have to make a big decision, I wait for full clarity. I wait for a sign from the Universe and an inner knowing that brings peace and a type of certainty. That doesn't mean there aren't difficult emotions that come with the process of letting go and even self-doubt, after the decision has been made. This is the process. And my faith and connection to my soul's inner knowing has become a reliable source. I ride the waves of my human emotions and processes.

And so, in June 2023, I let go of the physical space that is Allomi and said yes to this next chapter of the evolution of my soul.

ఆఆఆఆ

Chapter 7

Helping to Create the Shift

Waking Up and Becoming the Embodied Woman

Waking up:
A catalyzing event – spiritual awakening – dark night of the soul – realizing there is more than the "dream" you have been living

Remembering (the parts of you that you've lost touch with)
Reconnecting (through meditation, movement, investigation, contact made with lost parts of ourselves
Restoring (calling back all the fragmented pieces)
Integration (weaving in all the lost parts in daily practices, saying yes to the call of your soul... learning to listen... What does your soul long for? What did you love as a child? How can you begin to integrate these activities, behaviors, and outlooks into your life today?)
Reclamation (reclaiming, ownership, declaration... this is who I AM)

Embodiment (Standing in the full power of your True Nature... BEing... Feeling... Stillness... Power... Experiencing the integration of All Of You. You are here now. You are expressing all of you. Your life is a reflection of your soul's essence and purpose.

A Vision for the New

How can I keep the innocence of my pure heart, let go of the pain of the wounds, the doubt they created that still linger, and be with the wisdom I've gained while learning to open my eyes and use discernment?

It's not cynical or negative to be discerning. I used to think that. But only seeing the positive, only allowing yourself to see the good, leaves a whole lot on the table... a whole lot of unnecessary pain. So, I am opening my eyes to it all.

As I become willing to see, accept, and love all of me, it becomes easier for me to see, accept, and love all of you. And I can use discernment and make choices that feel empowered, embodied, and aligned.

Climbing Out of the Deep Well of Darkness

Climbing down into the dark well with others does not serve either of us. This is my pattern. I hang on to slivers of hope, because I see the little flicker of the soul self, and I want to pull them out from the depths of the hell they are in.

But I can't. That's not my job. My job is to be the hand someone reaches for, as they climb out of the darkness themselves. I can't go down into the depths of hell to get them... God knows I've tried.

When I'm trying to carry someone out with me, it's too heavy, and I give up and just decide to hang out there with them. It's too painful to crawl out by myself and leave them behind. So, I stay with them, and I suffer, and I lose the use of my gifts, because they don't work as well down there. It's too heavy, too dark.

But it makes me so very sad, because I see them, their sweet faces. I see their innocence, and I don't want to leave them there. But the only way I can use my gifts is if I am at the surface, in the light, reaching out my hand to help them lift out on their final ascension out of the depths.

It breaks my heart... Why is it that some of those I've loved won't fucking climb out? Why? I've tried to show them, teach them, love them, and hold them, climb out with them, side-by-side, encouraging them, but they refuse, and so I must go. There are too many others who need my help, need my hand. I will hand them back their pain, the pain I carried for too long. It does not belong to me. It never did.

It takes a lot of courage to open your heart, after you've worked hard to close it. It's so fucking brave. I had to shut down my heart, but I've always returned to this space of complete love, open heart.

It is time. I have tried too many times.... I will not climb down there again... I will walk freely. I will hold out my hand for those who are climbing out, both feet planted firmly on the ground, so I have the strength to help lift the weight of that last bit of their ascension.

I am here to help others make that final climb... The surface is so near, the light is so bright. They can see the light, and they have the will and the desire to make it out.

And then, we can play together... We are all lighter... And we can dance and sing in between the times where we help pull more out. But only when they have already chosen the climb and are close to the surface...

They just need that final help. They will be injured and weak, once they come out... It takes a lot out of a soul, being in that darkness for so long, but they will recover, and we will help them... Soon, they will be dancing and singing with us. Once they regain enough of their strength, they will start helping, too.

There are those who choose to stay down in the depths of hell and those who choose to ascend and climb out. It is not our job to make that decision for anyone else. They must make their own decision. We are just here to help.

I have spent my entire life climbing down, trying to pull them out, and I always get stuck, being down there. I drank alcohol, I did drugs, trying to numb the pain of being down there. I've always known my destiny was to fly... But you start to doubt yourself, when you haven't flown in a really long time and you've been in this deep well for so long.

The rest of my time here, I will play, love, dance, sing, and be a helping hand to those who are ready to climb out and fly with me. This is my true nature. No more dimming my light, climbing down into the well... No more. When my light goes out, I fail my mission. The only way I can be a source of inspiration is if I'm shining my light as brightly as it was meant to shine.

It is time. There is nothing to be afraid of.

❦❦❦❦

There is something very pure about my heart. I say this not from an egotistical place, but as the observer who witnesses my humanness. There is absolutely nothing broken about me.

I always thought there was something wrong with me, something broken, and that was why I was attracted to these wounded boys who hurt me. But it wasn't because I was broken; it was because my pure heart wanted to help them heal, and I saw their pain... They were the ones who needed love the most.

Somehow, I knew I was here to help people heal with my pure heart, with love. It wasn't because I was broken that I stayed with them and lost myself. It was because it was the only way I knew how to try to help them... I didn't feel like I could leave them until I'd helped them heal. And I had to go through all that pain, all that self-abandonment, so I could learn what doesn't work. But it was never because I was broken. It was because I knew my purpose was to help people heal. I just hadn't learned how to do that without losing myself in the process.

My purpose is to use my greatest gifts: of love and of being able to see through all the armor to a person's essence, but not get caught in the pain of their pain. It's like my greatest gift has caused me my most pain. I pray, from this moment on, to let go of that loop and only experience the love I give in its purest form.

I have seen wounded people and volunteered to carry some of their pain, and then I've forgotten that I made that agreement. I've forgotten it wasn't my pain, and I've lost myself in the weight of all "their" pain.

I was an actress, growing up. It's funny, because I feel like there have been so many times in my life when I've "acted" okay, when I was really struggling inside. I loved acting... I loved being able to purge my emotions without having to take responsibility for them.

I have awakened to a whole new world... A world where anything and everything is possible. My meditation practice reconnected me with the part of myself I had lost connection with... my soul... my higher self... The one who knows I AM here for more... The one who knows there are mysteries and miracles beyond what we see.

There is more to life than we allow ourselves to believe. We gather on the weekends, stuffing our faces and downing the wine, talking about how hard it is to be a mom and how our husbands suck... And this is life. We joke about it all, tight buzz, pouring more wine, convincing ourselves this is what our life is supposed to be.

But deep down, the voice is there... She whispers, "You know you are here for more."

My voice whispered to me, "You know you're not your best self in this marriage. You know this wine you are drinking is watering down the desire that burns inside you... Because, if you didn't, you'd realize this is not enough. And that is too scary to consider, so you keep playing the game, just like everyone else, trying to quiet the voice. But it is done being quiet."

Those first days of waking up gave me a sense of hope I hadn't felt in a long time. My daily meditation practice started to become something I looked forward to rather than dreaded. It felt like I was tuning into a secret that no one else knew. That secret has become my absolute truth and dependable guidance system. A passion and hunger for a deeper understanding took hold of me and continues to push me into greater and more fulfilling expansion and purpose.

In September 2018, I put on my first event, "Allomi Presents, All Of You: A Holistic Health and Conscious Living Summit," designed to ignite healing, inspire purpose, elevate consciousness, and shift culture. I had no experience putting on events… It was pure passion… It felt like a request from the Universe, and I said yes.

We screened the *HEAL* documentary, and Reiki Master Patti Penn, who was featured in the film, came and did a Q&A and taught a yoga & EFT tapping class. Amazing women came and spoke at my event, including the lovely Jill Willard, author of *Intuitive Being*.

I'll never forget my first conversation with Jill… I was standing in my unfinished space at Allomi, on concrete floors, staring at wood beams and dirt. I heard her kind and gentle voice through the phone.

"Thank you for saying *yes*."

Saying yes to the call. That's what she meant. It's not easy to say yes to the call, but it's necessary. It's worth risking everything. In that moment, I felt like she understood me, respected and appreciated me. This amazing woman appreciated *ME*, thanked *ME*. I am her, and she is me.

I had absolutely no experience putting on events, but I had a burning desire and a strong knowing. People said yes when I asked, and people showed up to support the cause. In that moment, Jill validated what I knew to be true, and it brought me tremendous comfort.

I am here to validate what you know to be true and encourage you to say yes to whatever your soul is calling you to.

ക‍ക‍ക‍ക

Writing Prompt

What do you have a burning desire and strong knowing about?
What does saying yes to your soul call mean?
How does that look?
How does that feel?
What are you afraid of?
Who would be upset if you answered the call?
Is it worth it? Only you know the answer.

I am here to tell you it has absolutely been worth it to me! I wouldn't go back, even if I could.

Being who I was born to be brings me everything I have ever searched for. It is everything. I pray you have the courage to say yes to your call.

ക‍ക‍ക‍ക

Who came up with the list of what is practical and realistic?

When you ask a child what they want to be when they grow up, what list are you referring to, when you say, "Oh geez, you should probably consider something more realistic."

Recently, my nine-year-old son had a school assignment. He was asked to write down his dreams... for himself, for his community, and for the world.

For as long as I can remember, my son has dreamed of being a professional football player in the NFL, like his hero, Tom Brady. My son is an exceptional athlete. He was born with natural talents and gifts, as well as an impressive sports IQ that rivals even the most avid adult sports fan.

I have always encouraged my son to believe in his dreams, to dream big and believe in himself. I have never once told him his dream was unrealistic and that he might want to consider a more practical dream.

When he shared his dream with his teacher, she told him he had to choose a "Plan B," because being a professional athlete is rare and something may happen to prevent it from happening.

I absolutely love my son's teacher. I absolutely love my son's school and all of the faculty and staff. This is not to place blame at all. This is to share how limiting beliefs are born with the best of intentions: to prevent disappointment. Dreaming big is scary; being safe seems less scary.

My sweet son is a rule-follower, and he didn't want to go against his teacher. I told him how important I felt this was, and that I would send his teacher a respectful email letting her know he would be writing his real dream, not a Plan B dream.

His teacher responded lovingly and thanked me for my email. Sometimes, we just have to be willing to go against the grain and speak up. I felt really good about this teaching moment, and I could tell my son felt really proud to own his truth. If we don't believe in ourselves and our dreams, no one else will.

What in the world could be *more realistic* than the thing you were born with? To be who you were born to be? The natural talents and gifts you were born with?! The thing that has in it the ability to manifest what it desires? How can that be anything but *practical?*

We should listen to kids more. We should pay attention and realize they are here to teach us! They are here to remind us of who we are!

Who determines what is possible? What is likely to succeed? People who haven't succeeded, because they didn't remember who they were and believed in some false list written by people who didn't believe in their own success and possibility! People who have made an agreement to put the box with the dream in the dark and lonely attic, like a pair of jeans that don't fit, but you keep them in your closet in case, someday, the impossible becomes possible, when some crazy, unrealistic, impractical dream comes true, and you realize you can fit in those jeans again, and you can unpack that box, and you can write your own new list, your own new story and song.

I feel the call to create, and it excites me… It makes me feel alive. Have you ever grieved the loss of your own destiny? Of what you thought you were here to do, but think it's too late? Why do we think there is an expiration date on our destiny? It's our destiny… It can't expire… It can only be allowed or ignored. Have you ever ignored that little voice?

Trusting Divine Timing

Do not be attached to an outcome. Trust the heart's desire and the energy of the desire, but allow for it to unfold in ways you can't yet see.

I started writing my one-woman show, *Waking Up to All Of Me,* after I saw my friend Julie's one-woman show, on March 1, 2020. In perfect divine timing, I had committed to working with a healer and given up alcohol in February 2020, so I was energetically and spiritually aligned to magnetize this experience.

I hadn't talked to Julie in years… Isn't it fascinating that she reached out to me at this exact moment in time? We are all energy, calling in vibrationally matched experiences. I saw her show in March, Covid happened a couple weeks later, then I moved out of my house in June and got a divorce. Clearing out the old to make room for the new!

What was holding me back? What is holding you back? Beliefs. Fear. Fear of truly being seen, of truly stepping out of the illusion and stories. My story: wanting to be relatable so people like me! Fuck it! I'm so over that story!

I am here to be all of who I was born to be. I have always known this. And trying to resist my destiny and play small is a silly game I am done playing.

It's simple. I have been addicted to that story. Addicted to the loop. And I am done with that loop. I am here to create a great impact and to inspire others to be all of who they were born to be.

How the hell do I expect to do that, if I refuse to be all of who I was born to be?!

༺༺༺༺

Journal Entry - February 16, 2021

I love the sound of silence. I love how it feels to take a nice, deep breath and feel calm, feel home in my body. That's what it feels like… like I'm back in my body. I am embodied.

When I am stuck or out of flow or in fear, feeling anxious and eager to escape what I am feeling, I do not feel like me. It feels familiar, a place I've been many times, but it never feels like the real me. It feels disconnected. It feels like I'm so far away from this place of peace and calm, of loving silence, of hope, of freedom.

I've spent the last several weeks feeling this sense of disconnect, of stuck-ness. When I am in this place, it feels like I'll never return to the place of peace and hope and freedom. It feels like I am a slave to my humanness, my fearful mind, the illusions, the worry, the addictions to escape.

I haven't had a drink of alcohol in just over a year, and for the most part, I am free from addiction and compulsion... And in these last several weeks, another growth spurt. Although sometimes, when I'm growing, it feels like I'm regressing, like I've fallen completely off track, and I don't know when I'll feel like I'm back on again.

Recently, I taught a group of women about addiction... I told them it was a lack of expression... I asked them to dive into what wasn't being expressed.

I want to express myself creatively and sexually and artistically and lovingly. I am alone for the first time in a very long time. No man is the object of my attention and affection. No man to think about, fantasize about, wonder about, hope about. It's a strange feeling... It's an uncomfortable feeling.

I realize how much I love loving. I even think I love loving more than I love being loved. My relationships have certainly reflected that. Perhaps my next relationship will be an opportunity to love loving and love being loved equally... Imagine that! That sounds nice. New, like loving the sound of silence.

I dropped my kids off at their dad's today after school. I've had them since Friday afternoon. I love them more than anyone or anything I've ever loved, and I also loved dropping them off at their dad's today. This is not always the case... Sometimes, many times, I feel tremendous sadness when I drop them off. But I am learning more and more to appreciate the time I have alone, to be in the quiet, to be with me.

I've been grieving a lot lately. Grieving the loss of the family unit. Grieving the loss of all the things a family does together. I've let myself feel the sadness, the grief, the loneliness. And today, I feel okay. I feel calm and hopeful. I feel like I've come back to my body, come back to my true self (embodied). It always feels like this, like I've been disconnected, having an out-of-body experience, and then I return, I always return, and I am always relieved that, once again, I have returned.

❦❦❦❦

Creating A New Reality Based on Personal Truth And Sovereignty

In my perfect world, I teach, lead workshops, speak, create, entertain, travel. I love to express myself through dance, storytelling, singing, being on stage, creating a project, an event, a show. I love the creative expression that writing allows.

I love the feeling of freedom and of infinite possibilities. I love living near the ocean. I love going for walks along the ocean. I love good talks with good people about things I care about.

I love my children. I love feeling like a good mom and practicing all the things this work allows me to be, as a mom.

I love being tapped into my innate sensuality and sexuality, activating my life-force energy and expressing from this empowered place. I love feeling courageous and taking brave and inspired action.

ৎৎৎৎ

Writing Prompt

What does your perfect world look like?
Allow yourself to dream.

ৎৎৎৎ

Journal Entry - January 2021

This last year has been a wild ride, and I live to tell about it with a smile on my face, gratitude in my heart, and a huge amount of hope for my bright future.

I gave up my wine (and all other alcohol, for that matter) a year ago; I left my marriage after fifteen years; I lived with my parents for seven months and started a virtual business, while my business has been closed for the last eleven months due to the Covid pandemic.

I just moved into my new home on my own, and I couldn't be happier. I am filled with the faith that I am always being guided and Divinely supported on this journey.

This new home of mine is better than I even imagined. My landlords are angels on Earth ... I believe with all my heart God has led me to them ... a soul recognition ... A Divine union. More people to love and support me on this journey. I am blessed. I am here to experience, embody, and express all of me, to expand into my greatest potential and to share my story.

This is freedom. The little ten-year-old girl is back, unabashedly, unapologetically living her truth and trusting her inner knowing. And this is just the beginning.

ഗ്ഗ്ഗ്ഗ

A Message From Spirit

"You've always known, you've always known, you've always known."

It keeps repeating as though it wants to make sure I never forget again.

"You are not crazy. You are a Divine Mother, here to BE love, to help the women remember who they are."

So many wounded boys who need to heal from the injuries they've sustained as a result of their mothers' self-abandonment and forgetting. The injuries keep getting passed down through the womb.

I've always known I am here to help others heal through love. I am in full remembrance. My gift, as a woman, is honest, open, intuitive, and emotional communication... I can stay in this open place, connected to my gifts.

My daughter Dawson was the fire who helped me remember my strength. And my son Will helped me remember the fullness of my mission. I am here to BE Love.

I no longer feel broken and injured. My spirit has recovered from being in the darkness. I help others through being a container of love. In this container, they recognize themselves. They begin to remember. This is why I am here.

So, I will fly... My once-clipped wings have grown, and I am no longer confined by the small cage I haven't dared to leave.

I will model for my children a life of freedom and expansion and will help them remember they are here to fly.

That, in fact, they already know how to fly... I can just simply love them and allow them to do what they already know how to do.

Over the years, I toughened up. I hardened; pain had me close my heart, afraid to love. And now, my heart has opened again, and I can be the love that I AM.

We are all trying to escape the pain of forgetting. And we ask ourselves, "Is this all there is?" because we know something is not quite right.

And the world says back to us, "Yep, this is all there is! And how dare you even ask?"

And so, we gather together to escape the pain of forgetting, in bars, nightclubs, and restaurants... We drink and stuff our faces together... We are trying to experience the euphoria of remembering. But when we dare to question, we are told, "Have another drink." And so we do. We have many, many more drinks... And for a moment, we feel the euphoria of connection, of love, of possibility.

But then, we wake up in the morning, and all of it is gone, like a good dream that is not real. And we feel even further away from remembering. We are caught in this cycle of trying to forget that we want to remember, because no one around us seems to care as much as we do about remembering. And we don't even know that is what we are searching for.

But we know something is not quite right. Until one day, our soul says, "Okay, it's time. It's time for her to remember." And we begin to wake up.

Journal Entry - February 2023

Something is happening. I'm going to be on the Single On Purpose *podcast in March. Something is stirring and unfolding, and I don't know how the story ends, but under all the wounds, the soul knows the end of the story, and it's all worth it.*

Journal Entry - March 7, 2023

I spent the entire day today in faith... Feeling such confirmation and resonance for who I am and why I am here. My mission...

I have a mission, and if I can remember this and be in faith, I can do it. I can handle it. But when I forget and I think it's all up to me, when I believe I need to play the game I don't know how to play, I am catapulted right back into fear.

Ego vs. Soul... Ego always jumps to the worst-case-scenario... Soul always knows we are exactly where we are supposed to be.

Journal Entry - March 12, 2023

We all want the same things. To experience peace, love, joy, fulfillment, purpose, connection, and expression; to be loved and understood, to feel like we matter, we make a difference; to feel like we can trust ourselves, to feel proud of who we are, and to feel physically healthy and vibrant.

We want the same things… To feel like we are growing and evolving into our best selves, to feel like we are making a contribution, to have healthy meaningful relationships, and to be financially successful and abundant. To leave a legacy that is memorable and impactful.

༒༒༒༒

Journal Entry - April 11, 2023

Today, I feel heavy, like I'm lying under a weighted blanket. It's hard to move. My chest feels tight. Tears roll down my face. I feel depressed and hopeless. My eyelids feel heavy, my body feels heavy. I can't seem to access the light, the hope. Everything feels so heavy and dense.

Yesterday, I made the announcement to my teachers and renters that I am handing over the lease June 1 and letting go of Allomi as the brick-and-mortar it has been for the past five years. It felt so right; I had such clarity, and I felt excited about the possibilities. But today, I feel like I can't breathe.

Am I making the right choice? Who am I? Who will I be, if I'm not the owner of Allomi? I am taking this leap, and there are only hopes and dreams I am leaping into… Nothing tangible, nothing physical.

Last time I took the leap from HIP, I had Allomi to leap into. And although it was terrifying, somehow the burden of fear was lessened by my focus on building Allomi. This time, it feels more ethereal.

Ego is reminding me, "Who the fuck are you kidding? You live in a fantasy. Every time you come up with one of your cockamamie fantasies about these big, unrealistic things happening, they never pan out."

And Soul gently puts her hand on my shoulder and says, "Dear One, take a deep breath, and let the tears roll down your face. Everything is going to be okay. Everything is okay. Just trust and breathe. You know, deep in your heart, you are here to teach, to give, to be of service to the masses. Just follow your heart and allow things to unfold."

It's so hard right now, because Ego is so much more convincing. He has data backing him up... clear evidence that many of my fantasies have stayed in fantasyland.

ﻬﻬﻬﻬ

The leaps I have taken... selling HIP, opening Allomi, giving up alcohol, getting a divorce, writing and performing a one-woman show, letting go of Allomi, and saying yes to greater expansion, writing this book.

Holy hell, there was a time when I would look at someone like me and feel in awe of what I have achieved.

I need to remember this, remember how far I've come. Stay in the present moment. It's no small feat, and I have done it.

I have always been okay, and I will always be okay. I am taking more leaps. I am right on time and right on track to achieving my wildest dreams as the woman I was born to be.

⁂

Journal Entry - June 1, 2023

Today, I am losing my identity as the owner of Allomi, and I feel lost.

I'm writing this book... The actual book being done feels very far away... What's the ending going to be? A memoir of a girl who had big dreams and ended up living with her parents in Long Beach, because she couldn't figure out how to make her dreams a reality...?

Oh, this is fucking pathetic. A couple days ago, I was an embodied woman, so powerful and ready for my destiny. And today, I'm just me, single divorced mom who was a business owner and who now is just that little girl who always wanted to put on a show and be in the spotlight...

I'm taking this leap to be the girl who wants to put on a show and be in the spotlight, and I feel the weight of the world on my chest. I hear all the voices of how that's totally unrealistic.

When I'm feeling so heavy and afraid, it feels like I'm all alone, having to figure this all out, capable of making a huge mistake... I completely lose sight of having help and guidance from Spirit. I can't feel Spirit when I'm so stuck in my head, and I go down the rabbit hole of fear and doom.

Doom and dread are such awful feelings, not the vibrations that Abraham Hicks says I need to have, in order to attract all that is in my Vortex.

Journal Entry - July 2, 2023

Today, I am writing my book. I feel good about letting the space go. I feel calm. I am tuned into my knowing. I always get my needs met.

If I don't jump into the story and let it carry me away, down the river of doom, I realize it's just a circumstance. And circumstances change.

And clearly, emotions change. One day, I feel incredibly hopeful and clear. And days later, I am struck with a heavy fear of doom. None of it is real... It's all an illusion... It changes, like the weather.

We can choose to simply notice... Oh, look, it's sunny today. Nice. Oh, look, it's cloudy today. Nice.

Perhaps one is preferable, but it doesn't change who I AM. Emotions and fears and triggers come and go, but who I AM stays the same. I AM love.

I AM love when the sun is out, I AM love when it's raining. I AM love living in this house. I AM love living in that house.

I share these journal entries with you, vulnerably exposing my innermost private moments and thoughts, for the sole purpose of showing you that thoughts come and go, feelings come and go. One day, I feel on top of the world, and the next day, my old stories and limiting beliefs take hold of me, pulling me into doubt and darkness.

I share these with you as evidence that I always return to the light, I always return to hope. And I take inspired action in spite of my greatest fears. I keep showing up, asking for help when I need it and being of service throughout all of it.

For many years, I only wanted to share myself when I was in the light, happy, upbeat, and positive. I wanted to hide when I wasn't feeling good, fearing judgment. I thought I needed to be "inspiring" all the time. But I don't want to mislead the people to whom I am being of service.

Today, I see all of my experiences simply as the human experience. Nothing to be ashamed of; something we all go through—ups and downs, ebbs and flows. And it is my great wish to be an inspiration because of my authenticity and willingness to be seen... All of me.

It is my great wish to be an example: that it is possible to say yes to the call of my soul and be the woman I was born to be *and* have days when I question it all, wondering if I'm doing the right thing, feeling scared and alone, and releasing what feels like a lifetime of tears.

My resilience always shows up... It never fails me... My soul never fails me.

֍֍֍֍

April 15, 2023 - The Great Mother Poem

I AM The Great Mother
I AM Love
I AM Life
I AM The Great Mother
My gifts are love and birth and holding space and nurturing and making you feel safe. I can hold you in my arms or simply hold you in my gaze, and everything disappears and you feel safe.
I AM that powerful
The Great Mother

I feel the pain of all who forgot the Truth of who they are

It is our love, our beautiful hearts that can save the world.

There is nothing to be afraid of. We are Love. This world needs our love. Our arms open wide, our hearts open wide, our eyes open wide.

Let us do what we are born to do.

We wish to BE in our power.

We wish to love you and hold you in our powerful arms and powerful gaze.

And when you allow this love to penetrate, it is Magic.

We are Magic.

These are our gifts.

Can't you see?

A world where we spread our arms wide open, fingertips to fingertips. Can you feel it?

There is no need for you to diminish your power. No need to dim your light. We can all shine, we all MUST shine!

We are here to light up the world

We are the Great Mothers who are remembering

And our Great Daughters will never forget

Because we will not allow that to happen ever again!

They are so bright... so many of them... beautiful, bright, fierce

This is why we are here. This is why we came.

A New Earth

Where I AM all of me

And you are all of you

Will you join me?

I have come here at this time to be the Embodied Woman... the Great Mother and the Divine Feminine. The pure innocence of the little girl, and the heartbroken, wounded teenager who didn't understand, and the heart that continued to love even when it was broken.

I am the woman who tried to be hard, because that is what the world told me was safe, and I am the woman who is soft, because that is my true nature. I am powerful beyond measure, and yet I still carry the wounds of my past.

They try to make me forget... but I have already remembered. The Great Mother, The Embodied Woman... She is here; she will not allow me to forget ever again. She saves me over and over.

There are times when I want to give up. I want to crawl in a hole and cry... And I have... and I do... But that is not why I came here.

I must continue, because I came here for a very important reason. We all have. Let us all help one another remember and teach one another how never to forget.

A Message from Spirit

If we knew how truly magnificent we were, and if we could see what "they" see, we would never, ever be afraid of money not coming... We are brilliant, and our only job is to shine our light and be authentic. The rest will take care of itself.

Journal Entry - May 12, 2023

I can feel myself now, having slid into this next higher version, embodying the woman who is my destiny...I am liberated. I am free. It doesn't feel so far away, the stage, the large audience, the money, the ocean-view home, the acknowledgment and invitations, offerings and opportunities... It feels so close, and it is not yet what I am experiencing in this physical reality completely... So close... I am in the body, just waiting for the experiences to come into view, for the vision to manifest.

I have been to the future and back. I have seen my future self, been in her body, felt her experiences, and now it is a matter of allowing. When the voices of doubt creep it, which, undoubtedly, they will, because Ego doesn't go down without a fight... I will carry on. I have the tools. I am resilient. I have been to hell and back many times.

Does everyone experience this? It seems so dramatic, when I read it outside of the darkness. But when I'm in it, it feels so real, so unrelenting and real.

Recently, I heard spiritual teacher and author of Don't Keep your Day Job, *Cathy Heller*, talk about some of the great spiritual teachers we admire, like Eckhart Tolle and Katie Byron, having experienced homelessness and deep, dark depression. The way she explained it took the shame out of it. It makes sense that someone with the capacity for so much light also has the capacity for so much darkness.

For those of us who feel called to teach, it is helpful to have experienced the spectrum of human emotion.

The road to inspiration is paved with acceptance, love, allowing, listening, receiving, and nurturing. We can move out of a depressed state into a more hopeful state by simply allowing ourselves to lie on the couch and listen to an uplifting podcast.

We are sent the right people at the right time, to help us on each leg of the journey. Spiritual teacher Cathy Heller is who has been sent to me recently. She is medicine, and she is resonance, and she is love.

And I AM love. She is reflecting that back to me.

❦❦❦❦

Journal Entry - June 13, 2023

Today, I'm feeling better than I did yesterday. I feel a little more hopeful than I did yesterday. Today, I'm giving myself some grace that it was only thirteen days ago when I gave up the Allomi brick-and-mortar space. For the first time in twelve years, I am not the owner of a brick-and-mortar studio, a physical space.

Today, I am not able to say, "I'm Amber. I'm the owner of a studio." I know this is my evolution... I know I made the right choice, and it's time for me to spread my wings and fly. I know we have to let go of the old to make room for the new, for all that I desire. And I am learning how much of my worthiness and sense of value came from the role I played, the label of being an "owner."

I know what I want to do. I want to share my story. I want to have deep, meaningful conversations about this journey to becoming who I was born to be. I want to speak. I want to entertain. I want to sing and dance. I want to express myself creatively.

> *I want to have a flexible schedule, so I can pick up my kids from school and take them to dance class and lacrosse practice. I want to travel. I want to step outside of my comfort zone. I want to make a lot of money and help a lot of people.*
>
> *I want to have a beautiful home with an ocean view, where I can host gatherings and day retreats. I want to teach and share and inspire and help people heal. I want to love and be loved, deeply and intimately.*

❃❃❃❃

I want to feel a deep sense of connection with the people in my life. I want to be a living example for people on this path of living their most authentically expressed life.

I know that my superpowers are love and compassion and empathy. I know my superpowers are being able to see through the masks people wear to their truth. I know my superpower is the ability to be incredibly honest and tell my story and be vulnerable.

My superpowers are to be magnetic and radiant and real. I know one of the things that brings me the most joy is loving other people, helping them to feel seen and known.

One of the reasons I wrote my one-woman show, and why I am writing this book, is because I want everyone to feel less alone. And because I've been through a lot of challenging experiences that I've come to the other side of, and I want to give others hope.

Authenticity, Alignment, Allowing

One of the many spiritual teachers I have been introduced to over the past nine years of my healing journey is Abraham Hicks and their teachings on the Law of

Attraction. The premise of the teachings focuses on being the creators of our reality.

We are energy, and our thoughts and feelings create a vibration. We have the power to align with the vibration of our desires by choosing better feeling thoughts over and over. I often refer to Abraham Hicks's "The 5 Steps to Alignment" as a tool, when I am wanting to come into more authentic alignment with my higher soul self.

Abraham Hicks: The 5 Steps to Alignment

Step 1: You Experience Contrast
Step 2: Source Answers Your Request and Creates Your Desire
Step 3: Align With The Vibration of Your Desire
Step 4: Maintain Your Alignment Consistently
Step 5: Appreciate the Contrast

Yesterday, I was feeling sad and lonely. I experienced Step 1: Contrast... I didn't like how I was feeling.

Step 2: My desire, born out of the contrast... My desire was to feel better, more hopeful, and less alone.

And then, this morning, when I woke up, I was still feeling a little bit tired, but also a little bit lighter. I went and took a class. I moved my body, and that's always good.

Step 3: For me, the vibration of feeling better is often achieved through physical movement.

More Step 3: Managing my mood by what I schedule in my day.

And then, I came home. I've signed up for this three-month program of Cathy Heller's, called "Abundant Ever After," because I want to be abundant ever after.

I start noticing limiting beliefs sneaking in: I still have this belief that it's lazy of me, or I'm not being productive, sitting at my computer, listening to the live calls. I have to take a look at the limiting beliefs I have around what is productive and what is going to manifest the outcome I want.

The truth is, I got on the call, and they put us into breakout rooms. There were four of us. I realized that this is in alignment for me: having these conversations with other women about what lights our soul on fire and what limiting beliefs we are noticing.

Achieving the vibration of my desire... Feeling better and more hopeful by saying yes to the experiences that feel good, that bring me into alignment with my soul self.

Step 4: Maintain Alignment Consistently

Focusing on what feels good. Allowing myself to daydream about my perfect day: If I could get up every day and move my body, dance and sweat, feeling strong in my body, and then have conversations with people that feel real. That feels really good to me.

I love being on podcasts. I love having my own podcast and having these conversations all the time, sharing them with other people who want to achieve the vibration of their desire. I love to inspire and guide women. I love sharing my life and inspiring other people.

More of Step 4: I decided to go pick up some delicious food at my favorite café. Limiting beliefs sneak in...

"You shouldn't get that, because it's expensive, and you're not making enough money, and that's irresponsible of you."

But then another voice comes in and overrides with, "You always feel good when you eat that food. It's so high vibe and made with love, and it makes you feel happy. And you're supporting your friend who owns the café, and it just tastes so damn good."

It also makes me so happy, driving in my car, listening to an inspiring podcast.

Step 5: I appreciate the contrast... The limiting beliefs that show me where I still need to grow. Part of mastering my energy is noticing the contrast, the limiting beliefs, and allowing myself to choose differently and align with the vibration of my desired state.

It's all quite simple, really. It just feels complicated when we attach to the emotions and let them take us for a ride. We lose connection with our authentic self and stop the flow of allowing.

My children are such blessings in my life. I look at them with such awe and wonder. I look at them and think, "God, you are amazing!"

And I don't think they're amazing because of all the shit they do. I think they're amazing because of who they are.

We forget that, as adults. We stop feeling valuable or amazing for just being who we are. We've been conditioned to believe we're only amazing for all the things we do, what we accomplish, how much money we make.

One of the greatest gifts this work, this healing journey, has given me is the gift of being the mom I want to be. I still fall into guilt sometimes, for the pain my divorce has caused my children and how my unconscious choices have affected them. But for the most part, I feel consistently good about the mom I am.

I really like how I'm able to show up for my kids. It feels good. I like that they feel safe with me. I like that I'm able to hold space in a very calm, loving way. My healing has expanded my capacity to hold space for their feelings, their pain.

When they were little, I was holding so much of my own pain and stress. I beat myself up for my lack of patience and for how uptight I felt. Today, I have compassion for the woman I was, and I am so very grateful for the woman I have become.

My plan is to follow my heart and soul, trust the process, and be the energy that magnetizes all of my desires to me.

Often, when we are in a rut, just getting out of the house and being present for someone else can completely shift our energy.

When we parent our children, we are also parenting ourselves. Often, the things we say to our children are things we wish someone would say to us… Our way of parenting ourselves, nurturing ourselves.

Recently, my daughter was feeling sad. It was her dad's night, and I was dropping her and her brother off at his house. She said she wished we could all live in the same house, wished she didn't have to go back and forth between two houses.

For the most part, we have all adapted to our new normal, and it's okay. But sometimes, we get triggered, and the sadness comes in an unexpected wave. Sometimes, I feel sad that I'm not in a house where the family is all together. It's not an outcome anyone who gets married and has children thinks is going to happen. But it does; it's life, and we do our best.

And so, when my daughter was having these feelings and this wave of sadness crept up, I sat with her. I was just there. Loving her, witnessing her, seeing her, acknowledging her, allowing her to feel her feelings without trying to change them or fix them.

This is what this healing work has allowed me to be able to do. She sat on my lap, and I held her, stroked her hair, and took deep breaths, hoping to bring a sense of peace to her little body. The emotions flowed, just like the waves in the ocean... growing, peaking, and then crashing back into the flow.

And in the container of unconditional love and calm, this is what happened with my daughter. When the storm had passed and there was calm, I suggested a bath, as bedtime was soon approaching. I could feel that she had shifted and was feeling better.

And so, I said, "Okay, sweetheart, you go take your bath, get ready for bed. I'm going to go home, take my shower, and go to bed. I'll see you tomorrow. I'll come get you tomorrow. I love you so very much. More than the whole universe."

I could feel the tension leave her body, accepting what was in the moment. I came home and felt really good about the mom I was able to be for her. I felt really good for being able to just be present and that I have this ability to be the energy of love and comfort.

There's nothing more painful than knowing you have caused your child pain. I have had to work with self-forgiveness quite a bit since my divorce. And I am getting there. Most days, I know I was doing the best I could at the time, with the level of awareness I had.

It's just like Maya Angelou said: "When we know better, we do better." And today, I do better. Most days, I am at peace with that.

It really is amazing how the energy of witnessing, allowing, accepting, and loving can change everything!

Alignment First, Then Action

Today, I was really being challenged with this feeling that I needed to do something, to take some action, make something happen. Then, I felt paralyzed because I didn't know what to do. And so, I meditated. I got still and listened.

I realized, in my meditation, that the times when I feel the most grateful or the most at peace are when I am being of service and being love. From this place of alignment, my doing becomes clear... And sometimes, there is nothing to do, just someone to be.

"Reach for a better-feeling thought."
— Abraham Hicks

I know this quote can be quite triggering, especially when you are in a dip. A better-feeling thought can feel so far away and can even feel repulsive, as you sink deeper into the depths of self-pity and hopelessness.

But I am here to tell you that all you need is a willingness to feel better. I want to share this gratitude practice I did one day, when I was feeling particularly focused on what wasn't going the way I wanted it to go, rather than on what was going well.

This was the writing process that took me from feeling quite discouraged to feeling grateful. When you're feeling down, just look for the next better-feeling thought by speaking out loud or writing down what you have to be grateful for.

Gratitude Meditation Practice

This gratitude meditation helped me bridge the gap between hope-less and hope-ful... Finding my way to gratitude by thinking of the last time I felt truly grateful.

At first, I couldn't think of anything I was grateful for. But then, I thought of when I first moved into this house, before there was any furniture and the acoustics were really good. I was in my bedroom, music blasting, dancing around and singing as loud as I could.

I felt so hopeful and so grateful that I had this home, this beautiful place to live, a fresh start. I was no longer drowning in my unhappy marriage, no longer living with my parents, and I had my own space. I had a beautiful home with amazing landlords, and I had money to pay for it. I felt so hopeful. I felt happy and free. I felt grateful.

And then, I went to the times when I'm with my kids and I'm able to take them to get ice cream with their friends. Or the moment when we were at Trader Joe's recently.

My kids are very aware of money. "How much does this cost?" they ask. And then, my son Will said, "Oh, never mind. It makes you happy to spend money on us. And you wouldn't buy it for us, if you couldn't afford it, right?"

I tell them it makes me happy to be able to take them to the grocery market and say, "What do we need, guys? Fill up the bags!" It makes me happy. It makes me grateful.

Then, I flashed to last night, when my daughter was sitting on my lap. It made me feel grateful for the relationship I have with my kids and for the Mom I'm able to be.

֍֍֍֍

I'm so focused right now on how I'm going to make money. Fearful old stories... Critical old voices. And the message I keep getting is... just keep being of service. You need to be of service. You need to show up, and you need to be of service... You need to be Love.

And that's what I can do. But the only way I can do that is if I am staying in connection with the truth of who I AM and who I was born to be.

It can feel counterintuitive, but the priority is always alignment then action. If action is taken from a place of force or fear, the truth of what you are searching for continues to evade you.

Manage Your Mood

I listened to a podcast recently, a conversation between Cathy Heller and Sheri Salata, author of *The Beautiful No* and former executive producer of *The Oprah Winfrey Show*. Sheri talked about her top priority of managing her mood and scheduling her days with inspiring and uplifting conversations, like the one she was having with Cathy.

Yes, another tool. Manage my mood by scheduling my days to include conversations that inspire and uplift me. Past conditioning tells me this is a waste of time, that unless I am filling my days with tasks that directly make me money, it is not productive, and I am "living in la-la land."

But this new way of living tells me that managing my mood raises my vibration, moves me into the receptive mode, and allows for the inspired ideas to come. This new way of living requires me to take action that is contrary to my old stories and limiting beliefs.

Take action in the face of the voices that shout at me, voices from my past, "You're never going to be able to make any money... Don't come running back to me when you run out of money."

These voices haunt me and inspire me to keep going, because I know they are only voices. They are not truth.

ଏନ୍ତନ୍ତନ୍ତ

Journal Entry - July 2, 2023

Today, I met with Wendy J. and had the most amazing two-hour conversation. We totally vibed, and I'm going to be on her podcast July 20. We have so much in common, and I left my meeting with her so fired up and in resonance. There are other women out there who want to do what I want to do, who have big dreams like I have and are Being Love and want to make the world a better place by simply being who they were born to be.

ଏନ୍ତନ୍ତନ୍ତ

Embodiment Challenge

Sometimes, we just need a simple task, when we're swimming in this space of uncertainty and self-doubt, the in-between phase, where we feel so overwhelmed and can't quite narrow down what we even do for the next step. And having a coach or mentor to be accountable to has always been an incredibly helpful tool for me.

My coach gave me an assignment. She asked me questions and reflected back to me what I was most desiring. My intention is always to feel more embodied, so the 7-day Embodiment Challenge is my task.

What makes me feel the most embodied? Write them down, get clear, and commit to including them in my day for the next seven days. Journal on all the times I have felt empowered and all the emotions that I have felt. List out all the things that bring me joy.

And for seven days, I'm going to create one to three non-negotiables, one to three things I do every single day for seven days that bring me joy and that help me step into embodiment.

What I have discovered is one of the things that brings me the most joy, helping me feel the most aligned and embodied, is to connect with people, share my gifts, and be of service using my superpower of love. And when I don't have the space to do that or the opportunity to share that, I feel this empty and lonely feeling. And I get stuck, because of old, limiting stories and beliefs, and I forget how simple it is to return to the vibration of my desired state.

"The key piece to understand is you need to step into embodying your most expansive life *now*, before you ever see evidence of it in your world."

—Cathy Heller

This is what I came here for in this life… to be a living example of someone who can reprogram their beliefs and manifest their dreams into reality.

Diving Into New Beliefs

I am diving into this pool of new beliefs. I got out of the old pool but am still dripping wet, with some of the old beliefs. I'm in the process of toweling off, putting on a new swim suit, and jumping into this new pool.

I've gotta dive all the way in. Not just put my toe in, not just go in up to my waist, but dive fully into this new pool, under water, completely submerged, and get used to swimming in this new pool of new beliefs.

Heart's Desires and I AM Affirmations

What are my heart's desires? What are my gifts? It's important to take the time to contemplate, to dream, to be in the feeling of my deepest desires.

I list the things that call to me, that light me up. Holding space, gathering in community, creating a collective, sharing my story, sharing my experience, and being a source of inspiration. Helping people change the course of their lives, to manifest their dreams into reality.

My intention is to manifest my dreams into reality and help women step into their full, authentic expression. I speak, I perform, I entertain, I lead retreats. I AM honest, I AM Open. I AM accessible. I AM vulnerable. I AM passionate. I AM charismatic.

I'm going to continue to do this, one day at a time, to embody my highest self. I'm going to relentlessly commit to creating new beliefs, new programming, and to let go of the old programming. I'm going to continue taking inspired action and doing what feels good for me and right for me.

All the naysayers and all the bullshit limiting beliefs tell me it's not realistic, or, if it hasn't happened yet, then it probably never will. I'm done with that. And I'm sure it'll creep in, because the voice of Ego loves to creep in. But right now, I feel good about who I am. I feel good about where I am. And I feel hopeful about my life shifting quickly in a very large way.

It's really remarkable to think about all the women I am connected with right now; we are all on a mission to make this world a better place. We are stepping into our true nature, the Divine Feminine. She draws her power from who she is, not what she does. And we've lived in this world, where the emphasis is on what we do. And so, as women, we've been trying to play the game that way. This has us not being in our full power, because our full power is connecting to who we are and the power of just BEing. Then, any doing that we do comes from the place of BEing: being in alignment, being connected to our true divine essence, who we were born to be.

When you're the one who has a vision of something that is beyond what other people can see, they say you're crazy. You are taking a risk on something they can't see. Hold your vision... It was given to you for a reason.

I watched the movie *Air* last night, about the birth of Air Jordans, a superstar shoe for super basketball player, Michael Jordan. This movie was about men who had a vision and a belief in themselves that was unshakable.

It got me thinking about some of the differences between men and women in our culture... The differences in our belief systems. As a woman, I have been afraid to stand out, for fear of other women not liking me. Do you think Michael Jordan ever thought, "Maybe I should just tone it down a little bit? I don't want to make these other basketball players feel bad." Hell, no.

He was like, "I'm gonna dominate and play my heart out, because I know that I have a gift. I know I was born to be the greatest."

The only way a person becomes the greatest is if they know in their heart and believe in their greatest potential.

As women, we're often taught to tone it down, to be likable and nice. Not too loud, not too bold. I've done this my entire life. Held back, so I don't upset anyone or, worse, be criticized and not liked. Belonging was always more important than living to my greatest potential... Until now!

Imagine if all the people we admire, all those who inspire us, had decided to tone it down a little bit, to dim their light to make other people feel comfortable. Who would we be inspired by then?

Remember this! People may judge you, but it's because of their fears, the limitations they put on themselves. People actually want you to live to your potential, so they can be inspired, so they can see what is possible.

You give people hope by being who you were born to be. You just have to be courageous enough to face all the limiting beliefs and old stories, and you have to risk standing out from the crowd.

"Courage starts with showing up and letting ourselves be seen. Because true belonging only happens when we present our authentic, imperfect selves to the world. Our sense of belonging can never be greater than our level of self-acceptance. Vulnerability sounds like truth and feels like courage."

—Brene Brown

Today, I show up and let myself be seen. It feels empowering and terrifying all at the same time. The way I inspire people is by being me, in my full expression. And people either appreciate and enjoy that or they don't, but it has nothing to do with me. If another person feels diminished in any way because of me shining brightly, that is a reflection of their own stories and wounds. My job is to love them, see them, and stand in my full, authentic power and expression anyway.

Who do you believe you were born to be? If you are truly honest with yourself, you know the answer. The question is not, what were you born to do? The question is, who were you born to be? What you end up doing will come from your true BEingness.

And if you tone that down, water that down, because you're afraid to be alone or afraid people won't like you, you will live a life that is less fulfilling, less than who you were born to be, and that is painful.

And so, in order to deal with that pain, you will do things to distract yourself, numb yourself, like I did. I tried to resist who I was born to be for most of my life. Because, deep down, I knew it was a risk. It would probably mean I was going to experience loneliness and criticism in some capacity. But the truth is, when you're in a group of people and not being true to who you are, you experience loneliness and self-criticism anyway, so what's the point?

I'm at a place in my life now where I'm committed to being who I was born to be. No turning back.

Sure, the voices of doubt creep in, Ego shows up, but I just tell him, "Listen, I'm doing this thing. I'm writing this book, I'm doing this podcast, and I'm focused on being who I was born to be. So, you just take a backseat for now. Okay? I'm not gonna listen to you. In six months, if things don't change, we can talk then. But right now, I'm going to put everything I have into being who I was born to be."

The Divine Feminine

In the 1960s and '70s, there was what has been referred to as the second-wave feminism movement. Each wave of women reflected advocating and fighting from the level of consciousness at the time, for the rights that were of the highest importance at the time.

Beginning in the mid-1800s, women fought for the right to vote, to matter, and to be heard. And in 1920, the goal of the first wave was realized, giving White women the right to vote. It wouldn't be until 1965 for the rest of the female population to earn that same right.

And then came the second wave. On March 6, 1971, an estimated 4,000 women, men, and children faced the harsh weather to march from Hyde Park to Trafalgar Square in London. They marched in solidarity, demanding equality for women: equal education, equal pay, equal job opportunities, the right to use contraception, and the availability of state-funded nurseries, so women could go to work, if they chose to or had to.

This wave was about equality. Women wanted to be treated equally. Women wanted to be recognized and valued, the same as a man. I was born in 1974, and this is the consciousness I was born into. When you are trying to prove you are the same as, worthy and deserving of being treated the same, as opposed to being valued and recognized for what makes you different, there is an energy of adapting and modifying, of earning and fighting for recognition and respect.

Some other interesting facts I discovered, researching the feminism movements, was that it wasn't until the year of my birth, 1974, that the Equal Credit Opportunity Act was passed, which allowed women the right to open a bank account in their own name and apply for a credit card of their own, regardless of their marital status. Before that women had to rely completely on their husbands, financially.

Also fascinating was the fact that women were not allowed access to birth control until 1972, if they were not married. So, you can see how many of the limiting beliefs and conditioning we are currently dismantling and deconstructing around our relationships with money and sex were born. Our power was intentionally stripped. We were punished and scorned for sexual behavior outside of a marriage.

As a woman, my sexuality, my sensuality, is my life force, my Divine Feminine power. It is evident in the way the laws were constructed that there were those who didn't want us to BE in our full power and have access to our Life Force Energy. We couldn't have a mortgage or own a home in our name until the year I was born.

This is the consciousness I was born into. These are the beliefs I have been passed down from the women in my lineage. No wonder they abandoned themselves and gave their power away... They didn't have a choice.

This is why women have fought so hard to regain personal sovereignty and power. And this is why I am incredibly passionate about being a living example of a woman who stands in her power and refuses to hand anyone the puppet strings ever again.

When my children were first born, I was the co-owner of a fitness studio. I felt a great sense of pride and responsibility to contribute financially and to be an equal partner to my business partner and my husband. I also felt the tremendous responsibility of being a mom and all that came with that role.

My ex-husband worked many evenings and weekends, often leaving me to care for the children alone. I was expected to contribute financially and take on the caretaking responsibilities.

There were many times when I felt like I was barely keeping my head above water, trying to prove my worth, trying to be the very best at each role I had taken on, and I felt like I was drowning.

Women fought very hard to have the choice to be more than "just a mom," to be given the same opportunities as men. I am grateful for all the opportunities we have now and for how far we've come. But what I would like to see in my lifetime is the recognition and respect for who we are as women, not for what we do.

I would like to see recognition and appreciation for the immense gifts and contributions of the Great Mother. We live in a time where value is measured by the dollar, but the value of a mother is immeasurable.

So many women I have worked with over the years have achieved tremendous success in male-dominated industries, and they have a great sense of pride in their accomplishments. And yet, they feel the consequences of imbalance, of adapting to the masculine way of doing, and of abandoning the feminine way of being. I am not suggesting we don't need the masculine energy by any means. What I am suggesting is that the gifts of the feminine need to be recognized as equally valuable. We must come into greater balance.

Women must feel safe to soften, allow, flow, and intuit. I dream of a world where the unseen gifts of the feminine are once again revered and honored. The power and strength of the fierce Mama Bear, the gentleness and immense capacity to hold the loving space of the Great

Mother, and the raw, wild, and sensual life-force energy of the Divine Feminine and Goddess.

We have evolved into what is now considered the fourth-wave feminist movement. Over the years, we have created change, and each phase is the next evolution of how we, as women, show up in our power. For me, and for many women I know doing this work, the phase we are moving into is less about being able to do the same job as a man, and rather more about being valued for the Divine mission we came here for. The freedom to do what our souls call us to do.

We are so powerful. When we are connected to our soul, when we are connected to who we truly are, we have the capacity to change the world. This is what I have been called to do. To help guide women back to the truth of who they are. And I believe this new wave of women is reclaiming their true, Divine Feminine nature. This is not just gender related but energetically, in the world, to balance the energies of masculine and feminine.

In earlier waves, rather than fighting to be honored for their true feminine essence, women were fighting to be treated like men. My entire life, I have lived in this energy of needing to prove myself, my worthiness, through doing. The women before I was born fought so hard to be able to give me these equal opportunities. So, in order to prove my value, my worth, and to honor their activism, I needed to try to be like a man, to play the game of life as though I was a man.

All of my gifts, which come naturally but have not been valued as much as they could be, are connected to my true Divine Feminine essence. My energy, intuition, creativity, sensitivity, sensuality, the way that I communicate, the way

I see the world, and the way that I express myself: these are my greatest gifts. They cannot be qualified on paper. They are the unseen and intangible gifts the world needs now.

One of the first books that found me, after I had my spiritual awakening in 2014, was *Circle of Stones* by Judith Duerk. This book spoke to me so profoundly, I could feel it as though I had lived it. Duerk speaks of a time long ago when "life was still sacred ... women were autonomous, empowered and revered ... women's insight and authority in things unseen was most valued." And then, things began to change.

> *The wisdom of woman, gained through her identification with her body, with the Goddess, and with the earth, was no longer revered but ridiculed and rejected. Once honoured as prophetess and seer, woman was now scorned. Her instincts and intuition, through which she perceived the elemental energies in the cycles of nature, and her knowledge of healing were rebuked and humiliated.*

Duerk tells of one of the "last nations to hold the Goddess in highest reverence and woman in a place of honor" was the small land of Elan, whose capital city was Susa (pg. 36). My last name is Susa, given to me at birth, a name I have proudly returned to, after changing it twice for marriage, and one that I will keep for the rest of my days.

Full body chills when I read this... It was a sign from the Divine herself. Somehow, I feel connected to this sacred time and obligated to usher in this new wave, where women once again are revered and honored for our greatest gifts... The women we were born to be... No more proving, no more adapting, no more denying our very essence in order to be valued and respected.

I am so very grateful for all of the waves and all of the powerful women who came before me, and now, I gratefully accept my mission and live by example to the best of my ability... Embodying the Great Mother, the Divine Feminine... All of Me... All of Her.

To return to my true, authentic, Divine essence. To be in flow, to follow my intuition, to create something from my heart and my soul, and to help other people tap into their natural divine essence.

In order to live a life that is most aligned and most fulfilling, I actually need all parts of me. Even the parts of me that I have tried, most of my life, to avoid and change... The parts of me I have felt great shame around.

The voices of my ego try to fight their way in. "What if I'm wrong? What if it's all bullshit? What if I am just a dreamer who doesn't live in reality? You believe in a utopia that doesn't exist!" And my soul reminds me, the people who are the happiest and most fulfilled took risks, listened to their hearts, and "failed" the most.

The people who project onto you these limiting beliefs, who accuse you of believing in a world that doesn't exist, have chosen to settle. They have ignored the call of their soul.

ৎ৩ৎ৩ৎ৩ৎ৩

Writing Prompt

Imagine being born into a world that tells you, "The number-one priority of this life is to grow and expand."
How would that change the choices you've made?
How would that change the beliefs you have?

ஒ~ஒ~ஒ~ஒ

What is the definition of failure? What is the definition of success?

We have been conditioned to believe in a certain definition. We are taught that success is having one life-long partner and being married for many years… the more years, the more success.

We are also taught that being at the same job for many years makes someone successful. There is no room in these definitions for expansion and growth. In this definition, even if a person is wildly unhappy at said job or in said relationship, if they choose to leave, they are a failure.

By this definition, I am a massive failure.

However, if we are truly here for the evolution of our soul, which is what I have come to believe, then anything that contributes to our soul's growth and expansion is a successful endeavor. And the more we grow and expand, the possibility increases of things in our lives falling out of alignment.

By this definition, I am a massive success.

I feel myself moving into this space where I'm allowing myself to be witnessed… To be seen.

My one-woman show, *Waking Up to All Of Me*, is the story of me returning to me, giving myself permission to be the star, to shine my light, to be center stage, to share all of who I am. And also, to tell my story, because I think it's a really valuable story. And, I think it's very, very common.

The theme of dimming my light and abandoning myself so I could fit in with others is a pattern that I continued over and over again. It's painful, trying to adapt in order to belong, and betraying yourself. And we don't really always know that we're doing this. It is survival. I just wanted to fit in so much. I just wanted people to like me so much.

Dr. Gabor Maté's work about attachment and authenticity has been very profound and validating on my journey. I found his work after I wrote my one-woman show and felt so validated to understand how and why my choices were a result of this human dilemma. It became so clear to me, and my show perfectly displayed how this shows up in our lives. As Dr. Maté states, as soon as our authenticity threatens our attachment, we abandon our need to be authentic in order to be accepted in our tribe.

You are remembering. You are here to remember and then help all the other women who come to remember. You were born to fly, so let go of the cage and fly. We all have an invisible cage, and it's time to deconstruct and say yes to what our soul has called us to do. And when we do that, we begin to experience awe and wonder once again, and life becomes magical.

I am ready to let the world see me in all my power, all my light, all my authenticity. I refuse to dim my light and play small. I am spreading my wings and flying the way I was born to. A little more each phase of my growth... A little more comfortable being all of me, as I continue to expand. It feels really empowering. It feels like who I was born to be.

I have an opportunity to rewrite the story, to create my movie. I don't know exactly what the future holds. But I know that I'm going to stay the course. I know that I'm going to continue saying yes each time my soul calls me.

I wrote this book, I'm hosting my podcast, leading retreats, teaching empowered dance, coaching, and speaking... Doing all the things that light me up and give my life meaning and purpose. I am using my gifts in a way that feels aligned.

I have been divorced for three and a half years, and I have learned how to co-parent really well... Much better than I could have possibly predicted at the time. This is a good reminder... Everything always works out better than we imagine. And most of the time, what we fear doesn't come to pass.

I have handled the post-divorce challenges, for the most part, with grace and strength. My children are thriving; they feel safe and loved. I have become my own refuge, and I am teaching them how to do that for themselves, as well, through my example.

Life is a marathon. I will continue to be on this journey for the rest of my life here on planet Earth. But on this part of the marathon, I have reached the finish line. I wrote the book I have been wanting to write for years. I did it.

There is something so incredibly fulfilling about completing a soul assignment... And there is always another assignment... Always something more to create.

৵৵৵৵

Acknowledgments

I would like to thank you, my dear reader, for saying yes to the call of your Soul and for choosing to read this book. I see you. I honor you. I love you. May you learn to love yourself above all else and never again forget who you are.

I'd like to thank my mom and dad, for loving me with all your hearts and souls, for giving me a life you didn't have, for showing me what unconditional love is, and for always being a safe place to land. I am beyond grateful to have been born to two of the most special human beings on this planet. I love you.

Thank you to my sister Carrie, who, although you are seven years younger, has always been like a "wiser older sister." I can always count on you for sound, wise, and loving advice and support. You have always had a way of making me feel special and seen. I love you.

Thank you to my sweet inner child, who never gave up on me, and who lives boldly and loudly through me every day.

Thank you to my Uncle Jeff, for being my guardian angel in my darkest moments and helping me have the courage to ask for help.

Thank you to my amazing soul sisters and friends, and to the Allomi community, for giving me the opportunity to share my gifts and be of service.

Thank you to Christopher Lee Maher, for helping me remember who I AM. This isn't the first lifetime you have been a major player in the evolution of my Soul, and I am eternally grateful. Your gifts are medicine.

Thank you to my publisher, Samantha Joy, for sharing your beautiful heart and incredible wisdom, and to the Landon Hail Press team for guiding me with such love and encouragement, and for believing in me when I thought I was crazy for writing this book. Working with you has been a dream, and I am forever grateful.

Thank you to all the beautiful writers who courageously tell their stories and make this world a better place by doing so.

Thank you to all the courageous souls and spiritual teachers who have walked this path before me, saying yes to the call of your souls, giving me hope, and being living examples of what is possible. I am profoundly grateful to be in your company as a spiritual teacher, leader, and way-shower.

And, saving the best for last… I'd like to acknowledge my daughter Dawson and my son Will, the absolute loves of my life. Thank you for waking me up and helping me remember who I am. Thank you for giving me the strength to continue rising. Thank you for birthing the Great Mother in me, and for showing me how to love fiercely and deeply. You two are the greatest gifts I have ever known, and being your mother is the highest honor of my life. May you never forget the Truth of who you are. May you fly high and dream big. May you love yourselves unapologetically and unconditionally. May you be all of who were your born to be. I love you more than the whole Universe, forever and always, beyond infinity.

About the Author

Amber Susa is an entrepreneur, fitness expert, holistic health and embodiment coach, Reiki healer, inspirational speaker, writer, performer, spiritual mentor, and teacher. She is the founder and owner of Allomi (all-of-me), a sanctuary for holistic health and healing that focuses on movement, meditation, and mindfulness. She is the creator and writer of her one-woman show, *Waking Up to All Of Me: The Integration of The Inner Child and The Empowered Woman*, performed most recently at the Hollywood Fringe Festival, where it received rave reviews.

Growing up as an actress, dancer, and singer, Amber was naturally drawn to creative expression, storytelling, and performing. She has spent the last two decades in the fitness and wellness industry, passionately guiding and supporting people to optimal health and well-being.

After becoming a mother to two beautiful children, severe low-back pain led her to a meditation practice and transformational healing journey that has allowed her to become the woman she was born to be. Amber is dedicated to sharing her experience and inspiring others to live their best life. It is her desire and intention to elevate the collective through being all of who she was born to be.

Made in the USA
Columbia, SC
06 March 2024